P9-CEL-025

© 2020 Joseph Prince

All rights reserved. No portion of this book may be reproduced, stored in a retrieval system, or transmitted in any form or by any means—electronic, mechanical, photocopy, recording, scanning, or other—except for brief quotations in critical reviews or articles, without the prior written permission of the publisher.

Cover design by 22 Media Pte Ltd.

Cover copyright © 2020 by 22 Media Pte Ltd.

Illustrations copyright © 2020 by 22 Media Pte Ltd.

Scripture quotations marked NKJV are taken from the New King James Version®. Copyright © 1982 by Thomas Nelson. Used by permission. All rights reserved.

Scripture quotations marked NLT are taken from the Holy Bible, New Living Translation. Copyright © 1996, 2004, 2015 by Tyndale House Foundation. Used by permission of Tyndale House Publishers, Inc., Carol Stream, Illinois 60188. All rights reserved.

Scripture quotations marked MSG are taken from The Message. Copyright © 1993, 1994, 1995, 1996, 2000, 2001, 2002 by Eugene H. Peterson. Used by permission of NavPress Publishing Group.

Scripture quotations marked TPT are taken from The Passion Translation®. Copyright © 2017, 2018 by Passion & Fire Ministries, Inc. Used by permission. All rights reserved.
(ThePassionTranslation.com)

Scripture quotations marked KJV are taken from the King James Version of the Holy Bible.

Scripture quotations marked NASB are taken from the New American Standard Bible. Copyright © 1960, 1962, 1963, 1968, 1971, 1972, 1973, 1975, 1977, 1995 by The Lockman Foundation. Used by permission.
(www.Lockman.org)

Scripture quotations marked NIV are taken from the Holy Bible, New International Version, NIV. Copyright © 1973, 1978, 1984, 2011 by Biblica, Inc. Used by permission of Zondervan. All rights reserved worldwide.
(www.Zondervan.com)

Scripture quotations marked AMP are taken from the Amplified Bible. Copyright © 2015 by The Lockman Foundation. Used by permission.
(www.Lockman.org)

Scripture quotations marked AMPC are taken from the Amplified® Bible (AMPC). Copyright © 1954, 1958, 1962, 1964, 1965, 1987 by The Lockman Foundation. Used by permission.
(www.Lockman.org)

Scripture quotations marked YLT are taken from Young's Literal Translation. Public domain.

Scripture quotations marked ESV are taken from The ESV® Bible (The Holy Bible, English Standard Version®), copyright © 2001 by Crossway, a publishing ministry of Good News Publishers. Used by permission. All rights reserved.

All bold and italics in Scripture quotations were added by the author for emphasis.

Give Me This Mountain—Faith to Go from Barely Surviving to Actually Thriving

ISBN 978-981-14-5492-9

Joseph Prince Resources

JosephPrince.com

Printed in the Republic of Singapore

First edition

All rights reserved under International Copyright Law. Contents and/or cover may not be reproduced in whole or in part in any form without the express written consent of the publisher.

GIVE ME THIS MOUNTAIN

FAITH TO GO FROM BARELY SURVIVING
TO ACTUALLY THRIVING

A JOSEPH PRINCE
YOUNG ADULTS RESOURCE

THE ITINERARY

×

BASE CAMP 3
TAKE GROUND BY FAITH

>

BASE CAMP 4
OWN THE PROMISE

PREFACE

God has a special place in His heart for young people. More than anyone else, He understands what you're going through as you navigate your way through life in today's world. He understands the stress, anxiety, and uncertainty you must feel when you look at the state of your life—your career, your finances, your relationships. He understands the challenge of finding a job that justifies you taking that 5-figure student loan, especially when what dominates the headlines of the news and media are threats of war, natural calamities, the rise of terrorism, as well as new strains of viruses that threaten to upend the entire global economy and bring about massive unemployment.

In the midst of all these very real challenges, God understands the pressure on you to have your life all together. He knows that every day, comparison comes knocking through social media, making you feel like you're not achieving as much as everyone else and that you're being left behind. And He understands the toll that can take on your mental well-being too.

Friend, your heavenly Father doesn't just understand, but He also cares deeply. He loves you, and He wants you to know **He has set you apart from the world to be an overcomer**, even in these seemingly impossible times. You see, He has paid the price for you to have the promise of a bright future, no matter how contrary your circumstances, the news, or the latest statistics might be.

And so comes the reason I've worked with my young adults writing team to bring you this book. In *Give Me This Mountain*, you'll get to know your Daddy God's heart for you to go from barely surviving to actually thriving and learn how you can experience this reality when you **walk in His ways of faith.** It is by faith in the cross that you possess every promise in Scripture—His favor, His blessing, and His success in your life. And it is by faith in His grace that you are fortified with resilience, perseverance, and strength to face the setbacks and challenges that come your way.

My prayer for you is that by the end of these 4 weeks, **you will take on every day with the confidence and assurance that the Lord is with you and for you, with the resilience and wisdom to face life's adversities, and with the faith to press in and possess all of His promises for your life!**

In His grace,

Joseph Prince

INTRODUCTION

You were made to thrive in life. Did you know that as a child of God, this statement is irrevocably true? On days you feel like it is and on days you don't.

It's true on days when the doors to pursue your dreams get shut in your face, and you're left high and dry. It's true on days you're hit with anxiety so bad you don't know how you're going to make it through the day. It's true on days you feel like a complete failure who just can't get your life together.

On days like these, when it feels like you're barely surviving, the idea of actually thriving can sound like the pipe dream of someone who doesn't know any better.

But my friend, it's *especially* on days like these that God wants you to know He made you to thrive—not just survive—even on the roughest terrains of life.

I know it can be hard to believe, especially for you, a young person living in a world that's constantly telling you how unrealistic it is for you to think you can actually beat the odds. Whether it's the people around you, the news, or that latest report that just appeared on your feed, so many voices seem to reiterate that life is an uphill battle that can't be won.

While that might be true for them, it *doesn't* have to be true for you.

In this book, we follow the story of a man called Caleb who stood at the foot of a mountain that everyone said was impossible to conquer, and with a resounding, "Give me this mountain!", conquered it. He was a man whom the Lord praised for having a different spirit from those around him who constantly echoed each other's fear, negativity, and unbelief.

Just like Caleb, you have been called out and set apart from the world to be a young man or woman of audacious, authentic faith in the face of adversity.

In the same spirit of *chutzpah* faith that Caleb and others like him in the Bible possessed, we tackle the relevant and gritty issues that blatantly confront us today, endeavoring to do but one thing—put Jesus and His grace at the center of it all. Only He has the answers that can steady our hearts, sharpen our vision, and impart faith for us to surmount every mountain in our lives.

My friend, God wants you to know that while you might be faced with overwhelming challenges in an atmosphere of anxiety and cynicism, *that's exactly where faith lives*. Faith confronts fear. Faith confronts hopelessness. Faith confronts unbelief. Faith is there in the space between barely surviving and actually thriving, and it will take you from one end to the other.

Are you ready? Let's go.

HOW TO USE THIS BOOK

Over the next 4 weeks, you'll learn from Caleb's story and those of other men and women of God in the Bible how to live by faith day by day.

Weekly Milestones

This book is meant to be read across 4 weeks. Each week, you'll discover a new aspect of what it means to walk by faith and go from barely surviving to actually thriving.

- **WEEK 1: Made to Thrive**
  Discover the life of thriving God has promised you and what it means to take it by faith.

- **WEEK 2: Dare to Be Different**
  Find out how to live a life of authentic faith in a culture of unbelief.

- **WEEK 3: Take Ground by Faith**
  Learn how to practice walking by faith and claiming God's promises in your life.

- **WEEK 4: Own the Promise**
  Learn how to hold out for every blessing and breakthrough, especially when they seem slow in coming.

Own the Word

The Own the Word section at the end of each day's reading includes:

1. **A strong takeaway thought or action** to help you put into play what you've learned.
2. **Bible references** to help you dive into God's Word for yourself.

ADDITIONAL RESOURCES

1. ***Give Me This Mountain* Videostream Study Companion:** In this special video resource, you'll get 28 powerful **15 to 20-minute** video sermons so you can dive deeper into each teaching in this book.
   a. Follow up on each day's reading with a short teaching that will equip and encourage you.
   b. Gain a deeper understanding of scriptural truths from this book.
   c. Grow from faith to faith as you listen to the preached Word.
   d. Find rich, practical keys that will help you get the most out of *Give Me This Mountain*.

   Be sure to order this resource here.

2. 

"Give Me This Mountain" song: As you take a journey through this book, this is one song you'll want to add to your playlist. Be inspired and encouraged by this new song from New Creation Church's worship team, available on iTunes, Apple Music, Spotify, and all major digital music platforms.

BASE CAMP 1

MADE TO THRIVE

×

DISCOVER THE LIFE OF *THRIVING* GOD HAS PROMISED YOU AND WHAT IT MEANS TO TAKE IT BY FAITH.

GIVE ME THIS MOUNTAIN?

DAY ONE

GIVE ME THIS MOUNTAIN!

Give me this mountain?

What? That's the last thing most people standing at the foot of a 3,000-feet monolith with craggy cliffs and sheer rock faces would add to their list of prayer requests. Let alone a mountain defended by a company of well-trained and highly skilled warriors who so towered over the average man that they were called "giants."

Yet one man—after surveying this landscape of hard limestone and thick forests and after evaluating how an uphill battle against an army of mighty men on its steep slopes could turn out—said exactly that: *Give me this mountain.*

And he was 85 years old.

Think about the sheer audacity of Caleb's request.

And all for what? A promise God made him 45 years ago that he would conquer and claim this mountain.

It sounds extraordinary, but doesn't it also sound vaguely familiar? The realities that confront us in our everyday lives can feel insurmountable. You might not be standing before a physical mountain, but maybe you're facing a mountain of debt you can't pay off. Maybe you've hurt yourself time and time again on the rough terrain of failed relationships. Maybe you're overpowered by a host of negative thoughts and anxieties about the future.

And you find yourself barely surviving, hanging on by a thread to a promise you once heard. A promise from a good God that you would thrive—not just survive.

How did Caleb hold on to God's promise?

Where did his resolve and strength come from?

What was the source of his audacious, authentic faith?

The Bible tells us it's **the people who know their God** who will be strong and carry out great exploits (Dan. 11:32 NKJV).

At the end of the day, Caleb's story is less about Caleb and more about the God whom Caleb knew.

He's the game changer.

He's the giant slayer.

He's the faith giver.

He's the promise keeper.

And that's why Caleb knew deep down in his gut that with the Lord on his side, he couldn't lose.

Listen to what he said: "Give me this mountain . . . for you heard in that day how the Anakim were there, and that the cities were great and fortified. **It may be that the Lord will be with me, and I shall be able to drive them out as the Lord said**" (Josh. 14:12 NKJV). Check out the original Hebrew language this verse was written in and you'll see that the phrase "it may be" has no uncertainty in it. What Caleb actually said was, "**Since** the Lord will be with me, I shall be able to drive them out as the Lord said." Caleb was completely convinced the Lord was on his side. He knew that if the Lord had promised him he would conquer and claim that mountain, then the Lord wouldn't leave him to figure it out on his own but would back him up every step of the way.

Armed with the bulletproof assurance that the Lord was with him, Caleb was unstoppable. The Bible tells us, "By You I can run against a troop, by my God I can leap over a wall" (Ps. 18:29 NKJV), and that's exactly what Caleb did. He ran against troops of warrior giants and took them down.

UPHILL BATTLES.

He overcame the impregnable walls that fortified their cities and conquered them. All at 85 years old, when his natural strength and vigor were supposed to have run dry.

Friend, you'll find supernatural strength and confidence for the battles of life when you know that the same loyal, dependable, promise-keeping God who was with Caleb is with you too. Today He wants you to know you never face a single day of your life alone. He has promised that you will thrive in this life (Jer. 30:19 MSG) and be more than a conqueror in every difficult situation you're up against (Rom. 8:37 NKJV), and He is right there with you every step of the way to keep His Word. With Him, you can rise up with faith to go from barely surviving to actually thriving. With Him, you can stand at the foot of your own mountain and utter the same words Caleb did:

GIVE ME THIS MOUNTAIN!

OWN THE WORD

START A JOURNAL TO CULTIVATE
A RELATIONSHIP WITH THE LORD.
GET TO KNOW HIM AND HIS HEART
FOR YOU AS YOU JOURNEY THROUGH THIS BOOK.
YOU CAN START WRITING TODAY:

WHAT ARE THE AREAS IN YOUR LIFE WHERE YOU
FEEL LIKE YOU'RE BARELY SURVIVING?
TAKE SOME TIME TO JOURNAL TO THE LORD ABOUT
HOW YOU HOPE TO SEE HIM COME
THROUGH FOR YOU IN THOSE AREAS.
SHARE WITH HIM THE CHANGES,
TURNAROUNDS, OR BREAKTHROUGHS
YOU WANT TO SEE IN YOUR LIFE AS
YOU GO THROUGH THIS BOOK.

READ THE VERSES ON THE NEXT PAGE AND
WRITE DOWN THE ONES YOU SENSE
GOD SPEAKING TO YOU ABOUT AND
ENCOURAGING YOU WITH.

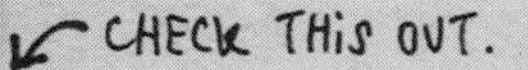

READ

JOSHUA 14:6-15 / JEREMIAH 30:19

ROMANS 8:37 / JOHN 10:10

ROADBLOCK.

DAY TWO

WHAT IS YOUR MOUNTAIN?

What is your mountain today?

For most of us, what comes to mind is probably the situation we're struggling in the most. It could be in the area of your finances, where you're trying desperately to pay off that student loan debt. It could be in your career or studies, where you're barely doing well enough to get by. Or it could be in the area of your emotions, where you're constantly overwhelmed by negative thoughts and fears.

It's true—mountains are often a picture of the problems we face. But in God's Word, mountains are also a picture of the inheritance we have as His children (Ex. 15:17 NKJV).

Yes, *inheritance*. In other words, all the blessings God has given to us through Christ. Blessings that are rightfully ours to claim, own, and enjoy.

When Caleb first laid eyes on his mountain, he saw that it had giants in it. But he also saw that it had giant-size harvests—clusters of grapes so huge and heavy that a single cluster had to be carried on a pole between the shoulders of two full-grown men. It was a land of abundance, and Caleb knew that God had given it to him and his people. That's why when he brought back word to everyone else, he said, "The land we passed through to spy out is an exceedingly good land. If the LORD delights in us, then He will bring us into this land and give it to us, 'a land which flows with milk and honey'" (Num. 14:7–8 NKJV).

Caleb didn't see the giant-populated mountain as a problem. He saw it as his portion. Years later, when he said, "Give me this mountain!", he knew there were exceedingly good things waiting for him in that land. He knew the Lord wasn't going to let any giant stand between him and the giant-size blessings that belonged to him.

Friend, your heavenly Father wants you to see your mountain the same way Caleb did. Instead of seeing the problems in your finances, your work, or your relationships as insurmountable challenges, see them as spaces in your life where He wants you to grow in—in your character, in your faith, in your ability to trust Him—so that you might possess the incredible blessings He has prepared for you in those areas.

Now you can be sure that **for every mountain you encounter, there is a promise for you to possess it.** It's your portion as His child, having been brought into His family because of Jesus' finished work at the cross. The Bible tells us that "every spiritual blessing in the heavenly realm has already been lavished upon us as a love gift from our wonderful heavenly Father, the Father of our Lord Jesus—all because he sees us wrapped into Christ" (Eph. 1:3 TPT)!

"Every spiritual blessing" means every single blessing in Scripture. These blessings include:

IN YOUR STUDIES OR CAREER — DOING WELL IN EVERYTHING (ACING THAT PROJECT, THAT EXAM, THAT INITIATIVE) PSALM 1:3 NKJV

IN YOUR FRIENDSHIPS — ENJOYING HEALTHY, NON-TOXIC FRIENDSHIPS AND RELATIONSHIPS (PEOPLE WHO BUILD YOU UP INSTEAD OF TEAR YOU DOWN) EPHESIANS 4:16 NLT

IN YOUR FINANCES — BEING FREE OF DEBT AND HAVING ENOUGH TO EVEN BLESS OTHERS DEUTERONOMY 28:12 NIV

IN YOUR HEALTH — BEING HEALTHY IN YOUR BODY, MIND, AND EMOTIONS ISAIAH 53:5 AMPC

IN YOUR PURPOSE — FINDING REAL FULFILLMENT AND MEANING IN LIFE (ACTUALLY THRIVING) EPHESIANS 2:10 TPT

As a child of God, this is what your heavenly Father wants you to hope for and expect to see in your life. Just like Caleb, you don't have to let your giants—the difficulties and obstacles that seem to be standing in your way—stop you from seeing the giant-size inheritance that belongs to you. This is your mountain!

OWN THE WORD

Think about the hopes and dreams God has placed in your heart. Think about the promises in His Word you want to see in your life. Are they already within reach? Or do they come with their share of challenges and obstacles? Spend some time talking to the Lord about them as you read Caleb's story in Joshua 14 and begin to see your mountain the way the Lord wants you to.

READ

Joshua 14:6–15

Candy Shop
Nickson St
ROAD WORK AHEAD
BEWARE of DOG

NOWHERE.

DAY THREE

CALEB CAME OUT OF NOWHERE

Yesterday you just read about how an 85-year-old Caleb took a mountain occupied and defended by giants. So you might be thinking, *This Caleb guy is unreal. He's a hero, a giant slayer, a man of faith. And I'm just . . . me. Me with my broken family. Me with all the pain I've been through. Me with all the scars people have left. How can I even hope to have the kind of faith that Caleb had? I'm nobody.*

If you can relate, then there's something you need to know: **Caleb came out of nowhere too.** In fact, we don't even hear his name mentioned until he's sent into Canaan to scout out the land. At this point, he's 40 years old. What happened in the first 4 decades of his life?

It's only when you trace the story of the children of Israel leaving Egypt and entering the promised land that you realize . . . Caleb was born and raised a slave (Ex. 3:7–10 NLT).

That's right. *A slave*. He wasn't born into a good family. He never got opportunities handed to him on a platter. He wasn't spotted, groomed, or raised to be a somebody. As a slave, he was a nobody. In fact, his name in Hebrew means "dog"—a spot-on reflection of the underdog he was.

But you know what? **God always roots for the underdog.**

The Bible says that "God deliberately chose men and women that the culture overlooks and exploits and abuses, chose these 'nobodies' to expose the hollow pretensions of the 'somebodies'" (1 Cor. 1:27–28 MSG). That's just who He is—a God of grace who's drawn to the last, the lost, and the least.

You see, that's the nature of grace, God's undeserved favor. Like water, it seeks out the lowest places. It finds us in the pits of our failures, our messes, our less-than-fortunate family backgrounds, our unsavory pasts, our bad choices. In fact, the Bible tells us **it's precisely the areas we've messed up the most that grace rushes into and superabounds** (Rom. 5:20 NKJV)!

Take some time to actually think about that. Think about the areas of your life that you always see as disadvantages or disqualifications. Think about the areas of your life that always make you feel lousy about yourself. Think about the areas of your life that always make you feel like giving up on the possibility of a bright future. These are the areas you can expect to see

God's grace flooding into and overflowing! And wherever grace goes, it brings restoration and transformation.

So it's time to stop allowing your weaknesses and shortcomings to deceive you into feeling trapped and held back from living the good life God has for you. It's time to stop making excuses to throw in the towel, telling yourself, *Things will never change for me*. Friend, nothing could be further from the truth because you have the grace of God on your side!

In fact, God's Word says you can even **boast** about your weaknesses, knowing that the power of Christ is moving in on them and overtaking them (2 Cor. 12:9–10 MSG). Instead of seeing your natural limitations and inadequacies as reasons to be ashamed or afraid, God wants you to see them as reasons to celebrate because they set the stage for Him to do a great work in your life. He did it for Caleb, the nobody who came out of nowhere with nothing to offer, and He wants to do it for you too!

So today will you bring your weaknesses, flaws, and shortcomings to Him? Allow Him to give you a new vision of how He can turn them around for your good and for His glory.

OWN THE WORD

After reading about Caleb's origin story, take some time to think about your own story. Are there things that have happened along the way that have left you feeling disqualified from the life God has for you?

As you meditate on the verses below, begin to see how God's grace can turn every one of your disqualifications into opportunities for His favor to work in your life.

READ

1 Corinthians 1:26–28 / 2 Corinthians 12:9

←There's more here!

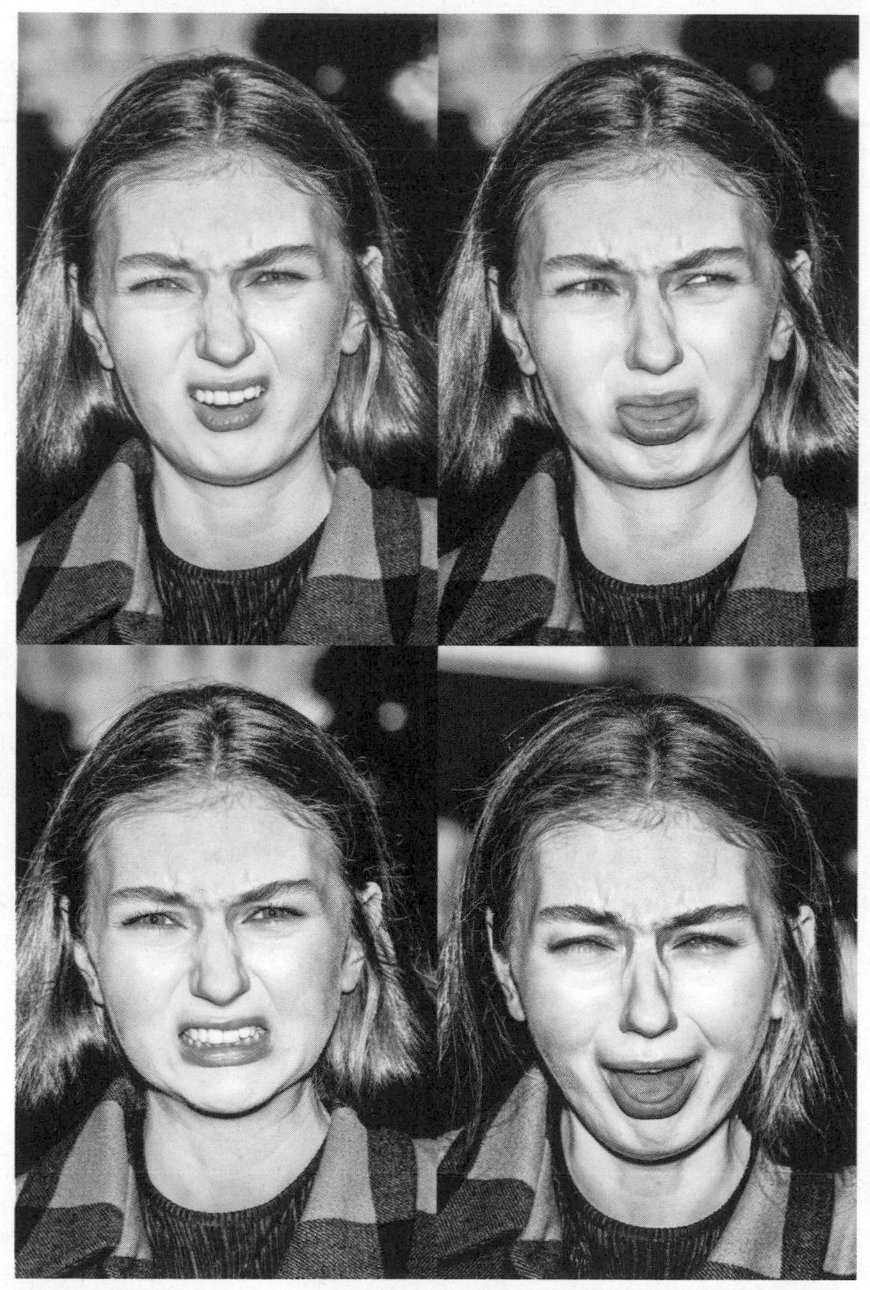

REACTIONS TO BITTER.

DAY FOUR

LEAVING BITTERNESS BEHIND

It's not always easy to expect good things to happen when you've experienced just the opposite time and time again. When you look back and all you can remember are your hopes being disappointed. When your heart is still throbbing with the pain of being lied to, taken advantage of, and hurt.

Did you know that when the children of Israel first came out of Egypt, they probably felt the same way? They had spent their *entire lives* under the tyranny of Egyptian slave masters. For years, they had been brutally treated, overtly oppressed, and heavily persecuted (Ex. 3:7, 6:9 NLT). It's very likely they had been psychologically bullied, lied to, and given promises of food or wages that were deliberately broken to break their spirits.

Imagine how their hearts must have crusted over with bitterness after all those years. Imagine how skeptical and cynical they must have grown. Imagine how difficult it must have been for them to believe anyone who made them a promise that seemed too good to be true. Even if that person was God Himself.

God knew this. And **He loved them so much He came down to their level of faith to win them over.** Do you know what the very first thing He did for them after delivering them from their oppressors was?

He brought them for a drink in the desert at a place called Marah. In Hebrew, *Marah* means "bitter." It was not only a reflection of the poisonous waters they found there, but also a reflection of the state of their hearts. When they tasted the waters, they recoiled and spat out, "So what are we supposed to drink?" (Ex. 15:24 MSG).

Now look at how kind and compassionate the Lord's response to them was in the face of their bitterness. He got Moses, Israel's leader, to cast a tree into the waters. Instantly, the bitter, toxic waters turned into sweet, refreshing drink for the people.

Can you imagine the congregation as they gathered around the pool of water for the second time? Weary from their journey and wary from one too many broken promises and bad experiences, they cautiously stepped up to take another drink. They scooped up the waters with their hands and brought it to their mouths, not knowing what to expect. Oh, how their faces must have brightened at the taste of the fresh, sweet water soothing their burning throats!

Beloved, this is what God wants for you. **He wants to make sweet all that's bitter in your life and restore your hope for good things to happen.** How? He draws your attention to the tree.

You see, the tree that was thrown into the waters is a picture of Jesus at the cross. It's a picture of the love of God demonstrated when He sent His own Son to the cross to purchase every good thing in this life. It's a picture of how Jesus willingly took our sins upon Himself so that we could take His righteousness—and with that live life with hope and expectation of abundant blessings. **Beloved, the cross is not only a picture of a promise made but a promise kept.**

Just like the people of Israel that day, when you begin to drink deeply of the Lord's love for you revealed at the cross, you allow His healing to begin where your deepest wounds are. As you take time to listen to sermons about His grace and meditate on His kindness and His gentleness, you allow His goodness to restore your heart and remove every sting of disappointment and hurt.

The Lord wants you to taste and see that He is endlessly, undoubtedly good so that you, like Israel did that day, might walk away from the place called Marah—leaving every bit of bitterness behind and looking forward to better things ahead.

OWN THE WORD

Disappointments and bitterness can be tough to confront. Find a good friend in your church group today whom you can be vulnerable with and begin talking about some of the things you are disappointed about. At the end of your conversation, ask this friend to pray and believe with you that the Lord will restore you in those areas.

Take time also to listen to sermons about God's love for you. You can start by listening to this free sermon **"Good Things Happen to People Who Believe God Loves Them"** at JosephPrince.com/gmtm. Scan the QR code to check it out!

READ

Exodus 15:22–27 / Psalm 34:17–18

#THESTRUGGLEISREAL

DAY FIVE

THE STRUGGLE IS *REALLY* REAL

The struggle is real.

Unfortunately, this is becoming less of a meme and more of a reality for so many today.

In a recent survey, nearly half of all young people in America said they've been through a quarter-life crisis.[1] Do you relate? It happens when you're overcome by intense feelings of anxiety and uncertainty from struggling to figure out your academic journey, your career path, and how your relationships will turn out.[2] It happens when all the steps you're taking and the doors you're knocking on don't seem to be getting you any closer to your goals. It happens when you look at your future and all you see staring back at you is the growing possibility of a mediocre, uninspired life.

Earlier, we saw how Caleb was born and raised a slave in Egypt. He was one of many. As slaves, all the Israelites knew was endless exhausting work, stress, and fear. The Bible tells us that besides serving their Egyptian taskmasters, even putting food on their own tables was tedious and tiring—they had to sow seeds and water them by foot (Deut. 11:10 NKJV). To get even the little they had, they had to do a ton of backbreaking work. It's no surprise that *Egypt* in Hebrew literally means "double straits" or "double stress."[3]

Sound familiar? Egypt is a picture of the world we live in. It seems like everywhere we look, we see people slogging away, working overtime, and losing sleep just to get that one step closer to their dreams. They're stressed out and hit with panic attacks because as slaves to the rat race, they think it's all on them to make it in life.

But my friend, **you and I are not slaves. We are sons and daughters of the Most High God, and He has a better life for us.**

In the case of Israel, He had a promised land prepared for them. One that was so rich and full of provision that it was said to be flowing with milk and honey! He assured them, "The land you will soon take over is a land of hills and valleys **with plenty of rain—a land that the LORD your God cares for. He watches over it through each season of the year!**" (Deut. 11:10–12 NLT). That meant they no longer had to do the backbreaking work digging ditches to irrigate their fields. All they had to do was simply plant and sow, and believe on the Lord to send rain.

SPIN CLASS.

Just like how the Lord brought Israel out of Egypt into the promised land, He wants to deliver you from a life of relentless demand and stress and bring you into a life of His abundant supply and rest. He wants you secure and confident in His heart of love for you, and He wants you resting in His promise to prosper you and provide for your every need!

Now rest is not inactivity. It's Jesus-directed activity. A life of rest is about keeping our eyes on Him and being led by Him on the inside. In all the work you do, learn to involve Him and focus on what He's leading you and prompting you to do. Only He can put you at the right place at the right time so that you can take advantage of the best opportunities that will bless and promote you!

Take a look at this beautiful picture of what it means to rest and work with the Lord: In Matthew 11:28–30 MSG, Jesus tells us, "Come to me. Get away with me and you'll recover your life. **I'll show you how to take a real rest. Walk with me and work with me—watch how I do it. Learn the unforced rhythms of grace.** I won't lay anything heavy or ill-fitting on you. Keep company with me and you'll learn to live freely and lightly."

Friend, God wants you to know that the life He has for you is so much better than what the world can offer. He wants you to know it's not all on you to figure everything out on your own. You can be diligent but without the stress, anxiety, and fear that keep you up at night. You can take one day at a time and be at rest. You can have a positive expectation of better things ahead. You can enjoy a life of rest, not stress.

Even when the struggle gets *really* real, know that your heavenly Father cares about every detail of your life and He is right there with you, watching over you and supplying His grace—His unmerited, undeserved favor—into every situation you step into.

TAKE A BREAK FROM YOUR FIRST-WORLD PROBLEMS.

Footnotes

1. "Nearly Half of Young Americans Have Experienced a Quarter-Life Crisis." Business Wire, July 17, 2019. https://www.businesswire.com/news/home/20190717005074/en/Young-Americans-Experienced-Quarter-Life-Crisis.
2. Ives, A. (2020). Putting The Quarter-Life Crisis Under A Microscope. Girlboss, March 15, 2019. https://www.girlboss.com/work/quarter-life-crisis.
3. OT: 4714, James Strong, *Biblesoft's New Exhaustive Strong's Numbers and Concordance of the Bible with Expanded Greek-Hebrew Dictionary*. Copyright © 1994, 2003, 2006 Biblesoft, Inc. and International Bible Translators, Inc.

OWN THE WORD

Draw a line down the middle of a page in your journal. On the left side, write down the demands in your life that make you feel squeezed and stressed out. On the right side, write down what the Lord is saying in response to every demand you've written on the left. Write down Bible verses about His unending, unlimited supply. You can find some of them in the section below.

Bookmark this page in your journal so that you can come back to it every time you start feeling the heat again. It will remind you of what is always true—that *God's got this!*

READ

Matthew 11:28–30 / Philippians 4:19
Proverbs 16:9 / Proverbs 21:31

← That's not all! Watch this!

CHOICES.

DAY SIX

WHOSE REPORT WILL YOU BELIEVE?

Have you ever tried listening to 2 people talking to you at the same time? It can be pretty confusing and hard to follow, especially if they have contrary points of view.

Now imagine not 2 but *12 people* throwing their opinions at you at the same time.

Sounds like quite the madhouse? That's exactly the situation the Israelites found themselves in when they were at the edge of the promised land.

Numbers 13 NKJV tells the story of 12 spies specially selected for a reconnaissance mission in the promised land to bring back word of what they saw. Can you imagine the scene that day as all of Israel gathered around these men who had returned, all eager to present their reports?

At first, they gushed about the lush land and rolling hills. They enthusiastically described the incredible produce and fruits they had seen—grape clusters so huge they needed to be carried back on poles.

And from there . . . their reports started to diverge.

On one hand, 10 of them started talking about the cities and the inhabitants of the land: how the cities were too well fortified to infiltrate and how the people of the land were men to be feared, ferocious in war and towering in stature. On the other hand, 2 of them gave a confident report: how they should all go up and take the land right there and then because God was on their side.

The majority brought **a report of fear based on the giants and the obstacles they saw.** The minority, Caleb and Joshua, brought **a report of faith based on the God they knew.**

The ensuing tumult that erupted in the camp of Israel was nothing short of pandemonium.

Today maybe you too are caught in the crossfire of voices and opinions between what God's Word says and what the world around you is saying. The news and the media tell you it's only going to get harder to make it in life. Well-meaning friends and family tell you your future all depends on you. And of course, the voices of doubt and cynicism borne of past hurts and disappointments tell you there's no way you're really going to beat the odds and come out on top.

What the world says	What God's Word says
"Look at all the instability and turmoil around us today. It's only going to get harder to make it in life."	You have a hope and a future because God has a plan for your life (Jer. 29:11 NIV).
"You live in a bad neighborhood, go to a bad school... where do you think you're going to end up?"	The Lord will make you the head and not the tail, and you will always be on top and never at the bottom (Deut. 28:13 NLT).
"If you don't have the right connections, qualifications, good looks, or money, you won't make it in life."	The Lord is with you and makes you successful (Gen. 39:2 ESV).
"Look at the family you grew up in. Your own relationships aren't going to be any different, any less dysfunctional, any less broken."	Your Daddy God will perfect everything that concerns you (Ps. 138:8 NKJV).
"You'll never be able to accomplish that. You just don't have what it takes."	You can do all things through Christ who gives you strength (Phil. 4:13 NKJV)!
"Don't raise your hopes. You're only going to end up disappointed."	Your hope will not disappoint you because God loves you (Rom. 5:5 NKJV).

My friend, God wants you to be selective about the voices you allow into your life. Whom you allow to speak into your life will inevitably influence the way you think and feel, the decisions you make, and ultimately, whether you thrive in life or not. That day in the ears of Israel, the voices of the 10 spies drowned out the voices of the 2, and with it, *even* the Lord's voice telling them that He had already given them the land.

The powerful truth here is simply this: **you get what you believe.** The sad outcome for the Israelites was that they got exactly what they believed—they could not enter the promised land and instead ended up wandering aimlessly in the wilderness. But when it came to Caleb and Joshua who took God at His Word, God caused them to remain strong, outlast the wilderness, and enter the land!

Today let's choose to believe the report Caleb and Joshua brought back: "Let us go up at once and take possession, for **we are well able to overcome it**" (Num. 13:30 NKJV)!

CROSSWALKS.

OWN THE WORD

What are some of the voices you've been listening to over the past week? They could be the voices of your family members, your friends, your boss, or a leader in your life. They could be the voices of the news and social media. Or it could even be your own voice. Take some time to take account of them and what they are saying.

With the Word of God in hand, begin to decide which voices you want to prioritize and whose words you want to believe.

READ

Numbers 13 / Psalm 1

OUT OF ORDER.

DAY SEVEN

STOP WANDERING. START WALKING

Let me ask you this question: *In your life today, are you walking or wandering?*

What's the difference? While they might look the same on the outside, there's a world of difference between the two. Walking is deliberate, purposeful, and advances toward a certain goal. Wandering is aimless, directionless, and makes no progress.

Maybe you've been feeling kind of blah about life, just going through the motions of the daily grind. On the outside, you might seem like you're doing okay, like you're making progress and moving forward in life. But on the inside, you're struggling to find purpose and make sense of it all. So what do you do? You put your head down, go through the routines of your day, all the while never really certain of where you're headed or if you're getting any closer to your destination.

Friend, God wants you to stop wandering and start walking.

God's plan for Israel right from the start was to walk out of Egypt straight into the promised land He had prepared for them. It was never His plan for them to wander aimlessly in the wilderness.

How did they end up wandering? Hebrews 3:19 NIV tells us the reason they could not enter the land was that **they didn't believe.** They didn't believe Moses, their leader, who constantly reminded them of God's goodness and faithfulness to them. They didn't believe Caleb and Joshua, who came back with a good and confident report after scouting out the land. They didn't believe the Lord and His promise that He had *really* given them the land.

Let's take a look at the journey of the children of Israel from Egypt to the promised land.

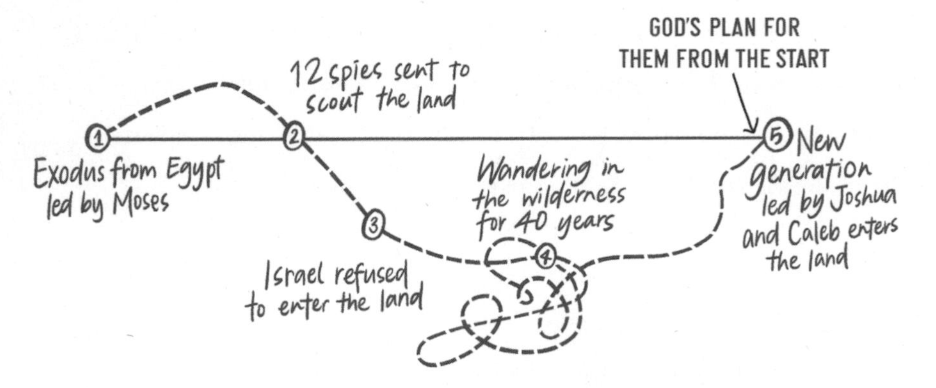

Can you see what happened to the Israelites? The old generation who didn't believe the word of the Lord ended up wandering in circles. The new generation who believed the word of the Lord walked straight into the promised land.

The same goes for us. **Every time we choose to take God at His Word and believe Him, we begin to walk. We begin to take ground. We begin to make real progress.** But every time we lose sight of God's Word and allow what we see to dominate our thoughts, emotions, and decisions, we end up wandering without any certainty of good to come.

Jesus Himself illustrated this with an insightful parable in Matthew 7:24–27 NKJV. He shared that the wise build their houses on the rock-solid foundation of His Word, while the foolish build their houses on the shifting sands of human logic and experience. When adversity comes, the houses of the wise remain standing, but the houses of the foolish are washed away. Friend, Jesus told this story because He wants you to know your life is too precious to be built on a shaky foundation that will cause you to suffer uncertainty and loss. He wants your life to be secure, founded on His unshakable Word. When it is, you'll live with the confident expectation that you will outlast all the storms of life and enjoy all the good God has promised you.

2 Corinthians 1:20 NLT shows us a powerful way that we can take hold of His Word: "For as many as are the promises of God, in Him they are **yes**; therefore also through Him is our **Amen** to the glory of God through us." This means that every time you read a promise or blessing in God's Word, every time you hear a preacher talk about God's good plans for your life, respond with a resounding "Yes!" and "Amen!" and believe God will surely bring them to pass.

Stop wandering and start walking into all He has in store for you today!

OWN THE WORD

Take time to journal to the Lord today and tell Him about the areas in your life where you feel like you are wandering. Tell Him about the fears, worries, and burdens weighing on your heart and mind.

Then spend some time looking up some promises in His Word that address how you've been feeling or that relate to the areas in your life you just wrote about. If you are not sure where to start, you can even try Googling verses: "What does the Bible say about my future" or "Bible verses about fear and worry."

READ

Numbers 14:1–38 / Hebrews 3:16–19
2 Corinthians 1:19–20

BASE CAMP 2

DARE TO BE DIFFERENT

×

FIND OUT HOW TO LIVE A LIFE
OF *AUTHENTIC* FAITH
IN A CULTURE OF UNBELIEF.

NOT DIFFERENT FOR DIFFERENT'S SAKE

DAY ONE

DARE TO BE DIFFERENT

Isn't it strange that of all the things God could have complimented Caleb for, He chose this one particular attribute, that he had "a different spirit" (Num. 14:24 NKJV)?

A different spirit. What could that possibly mean?

Is it just about standing out from the crowd? Or expressing who you are in the most unexpected and shocking way? In our culture today where individuality, self-expression, and divergence from the norm are celebrated and glorified, understanding what God means when He talks about being "different" can be pretty confusing.

Friend, God doesn't want you different for different's sake.

Look at this message that Jeremiah, a young prophet in the Bible, received from the Lord:

> *The* L*ORD* *gave me this message: "I knew you before I formed you in your mother's womb. Before you were born* ***I set you apart and appointed you*** *as my prophet to the nations."*
>
> *—Jeremiah 1:4–5* NLT

Today you're not different because of your personality, your clothes, or your lifestyle choices. **You are different because the Lord has called you and set you apart for His purpose!** The One who knows you fully and loves you perfectly has a glorious destiny for your life that only you can fulfill.

And here's the thing about the Lord choosing you for His special calling and purpose: He didn't choose you because of your natural abilities or qualifications; He chose you because of your weaknesses and need for His grace! Look at the reason God gave for choosing Israel to bear His name:

> *For you are a holy people to the* L*ORD* *your God; the* L*ORD* *your God has chosen you to be a people for Himself, a special treasure above all the peoples on the face of the earth.* ***The LORD did not set His love on you nor choose you because you were more in number than any other people, for you were the least of all peoples.***
>
> *—Deuteronomy 7:6–7* NKJV

DIVINE EPIPHANIES.

The Lord didn't choose them because they were the greatest or strongest, but because they were the fewest and weakest. It's the opposite way in which the world chooses people for their team because our God is a God of grace! So throw out the doubt about whether God can use you. He not only *can*, but *wants* to. Your minuses leave room for His pluses. Your lack leaves room for His supply, His strength, His anointing, and His gifts to flow powerfully in your life!

When you understand and believe God has a great purpose and plan for you, you can't help but live your life differently from the world. You don't have time to waste indulging in sin and meaningless pursuits that cannot satisfy. You stop living like the world—driven by a craving for physical pleasure, a craving for what they see and don't have, a craving for achievements and possessions that inflate their pride (1 John 2:15 NLT). Instead, you start making decisions and plans for your life that line up with God's Word because you know His Father's heart to lead you into a life that's greater than all these things.

It's interesting to note that in Hebrew, the word *different* that God uses to describe Caleb's spirit actually means "following." He said of Caleb, "My servant Caleb . . . has a **different** spirit; he **follows** me passionately" (Num. 14:24 MSG). You see, Caleb was different from his peers in that he had a heart to follow the Lord. And he did so even when he was sorely outnumbered 10 to 2.

Yes, there'll be times it might feel daunting to stand apart from the "safety" of the majority or popular opinion. There'll be times it might take courage to make a stand to follow the Lord in the face of peer pressure and society's ideals and opinions. But when you do, the Lord will stand up for you like He did for Caleb. He might not speak in an audible voice from heaven, but He will make sure it becomes obvious that your life is truly different and set apart for His glory. You'll find yourself walking in extraordinary blessings and experiencing real happiness and fulfillment that the world can only dream of.

Friend, the Lord is on your side, and He's calling you to be on His. Dare to be different!

OWN THE WORD

How do we find out God's purpose for our lives?

Ephesians 1:11–12 MSG tells us so beautifully that it is in Christ that we discover **who we are** and **what we are living for.** Because of our relationship with Jesus, the Holy Spirit writes God's plan for our lives on the canvases of our hearts (Heb. 8:10 MSG). This means the call and purposes that God has for you are often revealed in the God-given desires He has placed in your heart. Also, God's plan for your life will always be centered around what He's doing through His body ministry—the church (Eph. 1:23 MSG). So think about which ministry in your local church you can see yourself serving in.

Take some time to journal to the Lord about these desires today. You can start by having a conversation with Him around these questions:

What do you love or enjoy doing?

What makes you come alive?

If there were no limits, what is one thing that you would love to be a part of in the church?

READ

Numbers 14:24 / Jeremiah 1:4–5
Ephesians 1:11–12, 20–23

← Find out more here.

IN SECRET.

DAY TWO

THE SECRET LIFE OF A GIANT KILLER

When it comes to killing giants, there is probably no story more renowned than that of David and Goliath. How a ruddy-faced shepherd boy, barely 17, faced off with a battle-seasoned giant of a warrior with nothing but a sling and stone. The rest, as they say, is history—one little stone went up, up, up and the giant came tumbling down.

Like Caleb, David seemed to have come out of nowhere. Before his battle with Goliath made him a household name in all of Israel, David's life was nothing to boast about. It was actually pretty rough. As the youngest of 8 sons, David lived in the shadows of his 7 overachieving brothers, all jostling for prominence in the family, all fighting for approval in the eyes of their father, Jesse. Compared to his brothers, some of whom had already found their place in the ranks of the newly formed Israelite army, David seemed to

Jesse like nothing more than good help for the laborious and menial chores around the house, and in particular, that of tending sheep. One time, when the family was visited by one of the greatest VIPs in the country, the prophet Samuel, no one even remembered to tell David about it (1 Sam. 16:5–11 NLT). And no one, not *even* his own father, cared enough to notice he wasn't there.

Imagine what that kind of treatment can do to a person's self-esteem. Imagine the feelings of rejection and inadequacy it must have bred in David's heart.

Maybe for some of us, this hits so close to home that we don't need to imagine it. We get it completely. Whether it's our messy family backgrounds, the careless words spoken over us that made us question our worth, or the bullying we went through while growing up, we all have reasons we live with a constant sense of inadequacy and suffer from a chronic condition of feeling "not good enough" today. We oscillate between our desperate need to try harder in order to prove ourselves and our deep fear of failure that causes us to shy away when opportunity presents itself. Sometimes we even end up sabotaging ourselves when good things happen because somewhere deep inside, we feel like we don't deserve them.

So how did David, who was no stranger to neglect, rejection, and harsh words, become a giant killer? How could he hear Goliath's abusive taunts against Israel and not get triggered into inferiority and helplessness, but instead stand up with indignation and demand, "Who is this pagan

Philistine anyway, that he is allowed to defy the armies of the living God?" (1 Sam. 17:26 NLT).

What are we missing here? What was this young man's secret that made him unstoppable in the face of a giant?

We find our answer in the most unlikely of places and in what seemed like the most insignificant season of David's life—when he was in the fields as a shepherd boy tending his father's sheep. Having been basically kicked out of his house and sent to search out pasture to feed the flock, David could have spent his time rehearsing how he had been hurt, how his life didn't matter, how he was an insignificant good-for-nothing. And that could have very well happened . . . if not for the Lord meeting him there.

There, the Lord drew near to him and turned the fields of rejection into the fields of His presence, where David discovered that all the rejection he felt from his family melted away in the loving embrace of the One who had formed and fashioned him in his mother's womb (Ps. 139:13 NLT). There, David poured his heart out to the Lord and had the Lord pour His approval and affirmation into him. Some days when David was leaving the house, he might have heard someone yell, "Get out of here and tend those few, pathetic sheep!" to which David would hear the Lord say, "Come with Me, David. I love to spend time with you" (Ps. 27:8 NLT).

And there in the fields of His presence, **the Lord took down the first giant David ever encountered—the low opinion of himself** that had been built up over the years.

Friend, many times, the first giant in our lives that needs to be killed isn't in our jobs, in our studies, or in the "practical" areas of our lives. It's in our hearts. It's the same giant the Lord had to kill for David.

The world tries to deal with their self-esteem issues by practicing mindfulness and self-love. They look at themselves in the mirror every day and say, "You are enough." But it's their own voice versus every other voice in their heads, and their voice keeps getting drowned out.

But for us, God's children, it's a different story. **We have our Father's voice. The voice of the One who created us. The voice of the only One who has the actual right to tell us who we are.**

How do we hear His voice today? How do we meet with Him the way David did?

Jesus tells us in Matthew 6:6 NASB, "Go into your inner room, close your door and pray to your Father who is in secret." In Hebrew, the word for *inner room* has the idea of a secret place. Let me ask you this: What do we lock away in the secret place of our hearts?

Our hidden messes.

The things we don't post on the gram.

The things we don't know how to deal with.

The things we want to bury and forget about.

Friend, this is the room in your heart the Lord wants you to invite Him into—

where you keep all your feelings of rejection and self-doubt, where you hide all the scars left by people, words, and experiences. When you do, you'll hear His loving voice telling you how He made no mistake in making you. How proud He is of you. How He made you to be a champion in life. How no one else might see it yet but it's just because you're a well-kept secret that He'll reveal in time to come.

Friend, this is the secret life David had. This is the secret life the Lord is inviting you to share with Him too. This is the secret life of a giant killer.

When you say yes to the Lord's invitation, just like David, you'll find yourself running not away but *toward* every giant in your life that dares to try to make you feel small. Because you know the Lord's got your back and because you're just so done with the lies.

OWN THE WORD

For the next few days, begin to cultivate a secret life with the Lord. Find a place you can be alone with Him to talk about your feelings and things that are weighing heavy on your heart. Like David did, learn to pour out before the Lord your fears, worries, and things you might have buried deep in your heart. You can talk to Him out loud in a private place, write your thoughts and feelings in your journal, and even put on some worship music as you take time to hear His responses.

READ

1 Samuel 17 / 1 Samuel 16:1–13

PRESS MUTE.

DAY THREE

10x BETTER THAN THE WORLD

If you've been in church for some time, you've probably heard this phrase mentioned at some time or other: "We are in the world, but not of the world."

It might sound simple, but really, how do we as believers today live in the context of our world—its secular culture, its ever-shifting societal norms, its varied lifestyle preferences, and the online access it gives us to every kind of content—yet still hold fast to our beliefs and values as bona fide children of God? **How do we be spiritual in a secular world?**

There's no better figure in the Bible of someone who had to deal with this very reality than the prophet Daniel.

Daniel was born into a particularly tumultuous period in the history of Israel long after the time of Caleb, a time when Israel had rejected the Lord and as a result, fallen into captivity under Babylonian rule. There in Babylon, Daniel and his three friends were specially chosen and brought into the palace at the behest of King Nebuchadnezzar to be trained and skilled so that they could be of service in the king's court.

There they were. 4 Jewish teenagers thrust into the very heart of the Babylonian empire, left to navigate the unfamiliar and very secular landscape of palace life. As part of a select group of scholars, they had access to many concessions and even had wine and "delicacies" of every sort specially prepared for them by order of the king—delicacies that could whet any appetite and satisfy any craving. In fact, the king had mandated that they partook of these luxuries even if it meant going against their Jewish customs and beliefs, and going against the Lord.

Think about it for a moment. Daniel and his friends were in a foreign land and given such seemingly fine treatment and privilege. Far away from their Jewish friends and family, who would even know if they were to give in to temptation and compromise? After all, the king had already made refusing a non-option, didn't he?

There'll be times in your life when you find yourself in the very spot Daniel found himself in. There'll be moments when your values and convictions as a believer are questioned and even challenged. There'll be situations in which you are confronted with tough decisions to make in your career, relationships, and lifestyle choices in the light of the new "normal" society has adopted. There'll come a point in your life when your friends who don't know any better tell you:

"You only live once. Get out there and try something new."

"What are you doing wasting your time in church? Let's go get wasted."

"What's with all these rules? Just do what you want."

"Hey, it's just this once. No one will find out."

"How do you know you don't like it if you've never even tried it?"

"Why are you so uptight about premarital sex? Everyone is doing it."

"You mean you're still a virgin?"

Now here's the deal. God doesn't take pleasure in making it rain on your parade. Ephesians 5:11–13 MSG tells us plainly, "**Don't waste your time on useless work, mere busywork, the barren pursuits of darkness. Expose these things for the sham they are. It's a scandal when people waste their lives on things they must do in the darkness where no one will see. Rip the cover off those frauds and see how attractive they look in the light of Christ.**"

If you're reading this and have messed up in any area, it's not the end. Under the new covenant, you are a new creation, completely forgiven and righteous in Christ. You don't have to live a moment longer in sin or vain pursuits. In fact, the Lord wants you to pick yourself up and continue to shine for Him. By calling us believers the light of the world and a city on a hill (Matt. 5:14 NKJV), Jesus gave us a picture of how He wants to make our lives a testimony and glorious example to all our friends and family of what happens when He is real in our lives. He wants to set us apart with His favor and wisdom in such an immense way that we will end up 10x better than the world!

That's precisely what happened to Daniel. This young man was so conscious that his life had been set apart for God's purpose that he "**purposed in his heart that he would not defile himself with the portion of the king's delicacies**, nor with the wine which he drank" (Dan. 1:8 NKJV). So he went straight to the officer-in-charge, whom the Lord gave him favor with, and asked for permission for him and his 3 friends to abstain from the prepared delicacies.

God was so pleased with the choice these young men had made that He began to set them apart. Not only did they look 10x healthier and better nourished than their peers who had been eating the food assigned by the king, but God also gave them an unusual aptitude for understanding every aspect of literature and wisdom. God even gave Daniel the special ability to interpret the meanings of visions and dreams. At the end of their period of training, when the king interviewed them, he found them to be 10x better, smarter, and more capable than *all* the wise men in his kingdom! No one impressed him as much as they did, and so they were immediately assigned royal positions in his court (Dan. 1:15–20 NLT).

Friend, did you get that? Every time you choose to honor the Lord in the choices you make and in how you determine to live your life, God's blessing and anointing to prosper come on you. He will promote you and raise you up when you prioritize and give weight to His voice in your life (1 Sam. 2:30 NLT)! When His anointing comes on you, the result is not just some unobservable or "spiritual" transformation that only other believers can appreciate. No! The result is evident, noticeable, practical blessings that set you apart from your peers. God's anointing will make you 10x better than the world—in your looks, your character, your ability to understand situations and make good decisions—and cause everything you do to yield supernatural results!

Friend, you were not made for the world. You were made for the purpose and good works that God had prepared for you to walk in even before you took your first breath. Take it from the One who created you, knows what's best for you, and wants you to thrive in this life.

OWN THE WORD

The strength to live a glorious life for the Lord doesn't come from our willpower or determination. It comes from knowing Him and receiving His extravagant grace—His unearned, undeserved, unmerited favor toward us. Romans 6:14 NLT describes this so aptly: "Sin is no longer your master, for you no longer live under the requirements of the law. Instead, you live under the freedom of God's grace." **This means the more you understand the new covenant of grace, the more you are empowered to live holy and wholly for His glory.** The more you take time to meditate on how kind, loving, and full of forgiveness the Lord is toward you, the more you will find the desire for worldly things fade away.

Today take time to journal about and meditate on the moments you experienced the gentleness and kindness of His grace in your life. Thank Him and receive afresh a revelation of what it means to live under this new covenant of grace!

READ

Daniel 1 / Romans 5:17
Romans 6:14

WHO AM I *REALLY*?

DAY FOUR

MIRROR MATTERS

"Mirror, mirror on the wall, who is the fairest of them all?"

Most of us are probably familiar with this adapted line from Walt Disney's *Snow White and the Seven Dwarfs,* in which Snow White's evil stepmother, the queen, obsessed with being the most beautiful woman in the world, would utter this question every day before an enchanted mirror and wait in anticipation for its favorable reply.

While the idea of having a talking mirror that magically assigns you a score on some scale of beauty or perfection can seem like something out of a fairytale, doesn't it also bear worrying resemblance to our society today?

We live in a culture more obsessed with appearances and self-image than ever before. One that's constantly telling us what "the dream life" should look like, and in the same breath, how far we fall short. Social media and its ranks of influencers plaster our feeds round the clock with curated perfection—framing, filtering, and Facetuning the snapshots of their lives so that all we see are perfect looks, perfect relationships, perfect vacays, perfect latte art, perfect moments, and perfect lives.

Now if you haven't realized this about life and reality yet, perfection is pretty hard to achieve. We might think we know that, but the unreal and unrealistic standards on our screens still subtly and insidiously infiltrate our hearts and affect the way we see ourselves and our lives. With every scroll and every swipe, we feel smaller and smaller, and further and further away from what it looks like to be thriving in life. Every day, we stare into this talking mirror that tells us we don't measure up. Every day, we let it instill the perspective that we're not successful enough, not good-looking enough, not popular enough, not rich enough, not achieving enough.

The problem here is this: perspective = reality.

Jesus tells us in Matthew 12:35 NLT that the results you see in your life have everything to do with what's in your heart. So whatever the perspectives you have in your heart, they're going to play out in your life.

We see this in the story of the 10 spies who came back with a bad report of the promised land. Listen to what they said: "There we saw the giants . . . and we were **like grasshoppers in our own sight, and so we were in their sight**" (Num. 13:33 NKJV).

Wait a minute. How did they know the giants saw them like grasshoppers?

Did these spies, who were scouting out the land *in secret*, go up to them and ask?

Obviously not.

They didn't get that report from the giants. It was their opinion of themselves presented as fact.

The sad truth was that the whole time, the giants were *terrified* of the Israelites because they'd heard about the power of their God (Josh. 2:9–11 NLT). But it didn't matter what the truth was because the perspective of the 10 spies defined their reality. They saw themselves small, helpless, and a long way from ever possessing the promised land—and that's how their lives played out. They never inherited the land.

Friend, more than the reflection you see in the mirror, it's the image you see on the inside—in your heart—that matters. It defines how you feel about yourself, how you respond to unexpected situations that come your way, how confident you are in the face of your challenges, and ultimately, how much you thrive in life.

And while social media can help us stay informed and connected, God doesn't want us looking into a warped mirror every day and letting it tell us what to think about ourselves. He wants to replace it with another mirror—the 100% truthful and unchanging mirror of His Word.

You see, He has filled His Word with pictures that show you who you really are:

- If you've been seeing yourself as someone who's constantly struggling just to get by, Jeremiah 17:8 NKJV gives you a picture of yourself as "**a tree planted by the waters**, which spreads out its roots by the river, and will not fear when heat comes; but its leaf will be green, and will not be anxious in the year of drought, nor will cease from yielding fruit."

- If you've been seeing yourself as someone who's small and inadequate with nothing to offer, Judges 6:12 NKJV shows you how God sees you—**a mighty man or woman of valor.**

- If you've been seeing yourself as someone who's not pretty or good-looking enough, Song of Solomon 4:7 ESV reveals God's opinion of you: "You are **altogether beautiful**, my love; there is no flaw in you."

- If you've been seeing yourself as someone unwanted, someone who will never find anyone to truly love you, Psalm 88:18 KJV shows you how **Jesus bore the curse of rejection, being without lover and friend**, so that by the divine exchange that happened at the cross, you have the promise that **you will not end up alone.**

Friend, the more you behold these truth-bearing pictures, the more you allow them to infiltrate your heart and transform your reality.

The world tries to change their realities by doing everything they can on the outside to feel better about themselves—get on that workout regime, adopt this new diet, get a bunch of new clothes, gadgets, or things—and yet, inside, their deep-seated perspectives can stay the same. And so, sadly, they don't see the changes they're hoping for.

As children of God, our Father gets straight to the heart of the matter and changes our reality from the inside out. He gives us powerful faith pictures that change our perspectives and lives. And you know what? He doesn't just stop there.

Beyond compelling faith pictures, His Word reveals to us the *basis* on which we can own them. Behind every picture, behind every detail, behind every word in Scripture, is **the beauty and grace of our Savior who joined us together with Him and gave us access to all that He is and all that He has** (Rom. 8:17 TPT). When we open the Word and see Jesus above all else, it's as though we are looking into a mirror at the reflection of who we are in Him. We find ourselves completely and inseparably one with Him, and we see all that He has irrevocably superimposed on our lives. In these moments, when we are lost in awe of His glory and magnificence, we are inexorably transformed into His image—becoming more and more like Him (2 Cor. 3:18 NKJV)!

So friend, will you take up the mirror of God's Word today and allow your heart to be convinced that you are who He says you are and you have what He says you have? That's how you align your perspective with His and see your life transformed!

OWN THE WORD

Today let's try something really radical. Take a break from your phone and social media feed for the entire day and spend time with the Lord. Get out, take a walk with Him in the park, disconnect from the digital world. Ask Him to show you the areas in your life where you've developed an inaccurate or unhealthy image or opinion of yourself. It could be in the area of physical looks, your interpersonal relationships, or even your ideals for your career or future.

Write them down and begin to look out for pictures in God's Word that you can replace them with.

READ

Numbers 13:33 / 2 Corinthians 3:18

DAY FIVE

WIN OVER THE FEELS

"Quit being so emotional."

"Stop overthinking things!"

"Why are you always drowning in your feelings?"

Do you find people saying these things to you? That you're too emotional and always letting your feels get the better of you?

Well, the prophet Elijah had a rep of being emotional too. James 5:17 KJV tells us that Elijah was "a man subject to like passions as we are." Isn't it encouraging to know that this great man of God was just as susceptible to the ups and downs of life as you and me? Yes, at times, he could be full of zeal and passion for the Lord, but when things didn't go his way, he could also swing hard in the opposite direction and deep dive into discouragement, disappointment, and even depression.

When Elijah was on a winning streak, he was a force to be reckoned with. You might have heard stories about some of his greatest feats. Once, he proclaimed a three-and-a-half-year drought over the land as judgment against a wayward king. Another time, he had a no-holds-barred showdown with 450 prophets of the pagan god, Baal, at Mount Carmel, where He called down fire from heaven that proved to all of Israel who the one true God was.

Now you might be thinking, *Elijah sounds even more unreal than Caleb.*

But the Bible takes us behind the scenes of this great prophet's life and shows us that his lows were as extreme as his highs.

Immediately after his great victory on Mount Carmel, to our surprise and to his chagrin, we see Elijah running away petrified. What had happened? Queen Jezebel, who worshiped Baal and saw her prophets defeated, was furious at Elijah after what had happened and vowed to kill him. Suddenly, it was like all of Elijah's faith and confidence had been drained away, and he ran for his life.

How is it that just like Elijah, we can be so full of faith one moment and so full of fear the next? What is it about our human condition that we are so easily and deeply affected by what we see happening around us, so swayed by the ebb and flow of our feelings and emotions? How do we fall so easily into the troughs of sadness, melancholy, and despair?

Whether or not you've been clinically diagnosed or prescribed medication, all of us are human and subject to bouts of depression and low emotions. They can happen swiftly and suddenly—when something threatens our relationships, our families, or even our esteem. And they can send us spiraling, unable to control the flood of emotions and torrent of negative thoughts.

The Bible tells us that Elijah was so overcome by fear and discouragement after his run-in with Jezebel that he prayed to the Lord that he might die. He cried out, "It is enough! Now, LORD, take my life, for I am no better than my fathers!" (1 Kings 19:4 NKJV).

Have you been there before? At the point where Elijah was, at the brink of utterly giving up on life and wishing for the Lord to end it all? Or maybe even as you read these words, you're entertaining thoughts of hurting yourself and wondering if anyone even cares.

If you're going through a season of depression right now, I want you to know **the Lord cares.** He knows exactly what you're going through. He knows every secret struggle that in the privacy of your room puts you in depression. He knows the fears and anxieties that steal your sleep at night. He knows the depth of darkness in your thoughts that you dare not even share with your closest friend. **He knows it all, and He still loves you.**

Friend, in the midst of all that you're going through, the Lord is drawing near to you. He won't discard you because you're of no use to Him. He won't throw you aside because your life isn't a good testimony. No, the opposite is true. On your worst day and in your lowest season, He draws near to you and restores you back to life and health. Just like He did for Elijah.

In the day of Elijah's faith, God sent provision and sustenance his way through people and things. Once, He sent ravens to bring Elijah food. Another time, He sent a woman to supply him with bread (1 Kings 17:2–16 NKJV). But in the day of Elijah's depression, when he was running away and hiding in isolation, **the Lord Himself visited him to feed him and encourage him** (1 Kings 19:5–8 NKJV). What a beautiful picture of the Lord's gentleness and grace toward us—that in the frailty of our flesh and the brokenness of our humanity, His loving presence and promise to never leave us are never more real.

In the midst of your discouragement and in the moments of your despair, will you allow the consciousness of His presence to fill your heart? Will you allow Him to cause every fear to fade and every oppression to cease? There's a song in the Bible where the psalmist starts out describing the reality of God's presence with him in this beautiful rhetoric:

> *"The LORD is my light and my salvation;*
> ***Whom shall I fear?***
> *The LORD is the strength of my life;*
> *Of **whom shall I be afraid?**"*
> *—Psalm 27:1 NKJV*

In the last 2 verses of this song, he ends with this powerful encouragement:

> *"I would have lost heart, unless I had believed*
> *That I would see the goodness of the LORD*
> *In the land of the living.*
> *Wait on the LORD;*
> *Be of good courage,*
> *And He shall strengthen your heart;*
> *Wait, I say, on the LORD!"*
> *—Psalm 27:13–14* NKJV

As you do simply that—wait on the Lord and allow Him to strengthen your heart—I pray that you too, will not lose heart or give up, but be full of faith to see all of God's goodness come to pass in your life.

OWN THE WORD

A simple and practical way to have a blessed emotional life is to involve the Lord. Proverbs 3:6 AMP says, "In all your ways know and acknowledge and recognize Him, and He will make your paths straight and smooth [removing obstacles that block your way]."

How do you acknowledge and recognize the Lord when it comes to your emotions?

Let Him be the first person you share them with! Instead of immediately going to your best friend, your significant other, or your favorite group chat, go to Jesus. Every time something good happens, practice going aside to tell the Lord and thank Him for it. Conversely, when something less than good happens, also take time to let Him know about it and to pray about it.

If you're going through a season of depression, God wants you to know you're not alone. Not only will He never leave you, but He has also created the church to be His physical body and hands that are reaching out to you in love and support. I want to encourage you to reach back and talk to your pastor, leader, or counselor in your church about what you're going through.

READ

1 Kings 18:20–45 / 1 Kings 19:1–10
Psalm 27

THANK
YOU

CLUCK, CLUCK, CLUCK.

DAY SIX

COMPLAINING GETS YOU NOWHERE

Many times, when we go through painful seasons or situations in our lives, our first reaction can very easily be to lash out by complaining and blaming everything and everyone around us for our misery.

Simply put: when we are in pain, we tend to complain!

The people of Israel in the wilderness were no different. They'd been following Moses, God's appointed leader, toward a so-called promised land that was supposed to be fruitful and flourishing. But the reality they'd been facing every day was mile after mile of bone-dry, barren wilderness. They were weary, thirsty, and famished from their endless journeying. And so they started complaining . . . and they didn't stop.

They complained that they were hungry. They complained that they were thirsty. When God answered them by sending food from heaven, they even complained that He didn't factor in enough protein for their dietary needs (Num. 11:4 NIV)! In fact, they complained that He should have let them die in Egypt. They complained that what they were going through was worse than their lives in slavery. They complained to Moses. They complained to their neighbors. They complained so much they ended up wandering in circles, unable to enter the promised land (Num. 14:27–30 NIV).

Before we start shaking our heads and judging them for being horrible, ungrateful people, haven't we all let loose a tweet or stray comment when we were going through a tough time? Haven't we all ranted to a friend or in a post on our feed? Haven't we all, at least in the privacy of our rooms, let out our unfiltered opinions and pent-up frustrations?

Friend, while we all have moments of anger and exasperation that can launch us into a tirade of complaining, God doesn't want us to remain there.

In 1 Chronicles 4:9–10 NKJV, the Bible gives us a brief account of a man called Jabez. He was a man well acquainted with pain, so much so that his name literally means "pain" or "sorrow." His mother gave him that name because of the extreme labor she had to endure when she gave birth to him. Jabez's name came to characterize his life. He lived his life in a cycle of causing pain and receiving pain. It was a miserable existence. If anyone had the right to complain about their lot in life, it was him.

But that was not what Jabez did. Instead of complaining or being upset with life, his family, his situation, or God, Jabez did something completely unexpected. Something counterintuitive to human nature and the culture around him. Something so simple, yet so powerful.

He asked the Lord to bless him.

He asked the Lord to disrupt his cycle of pain with His hand of blessing. Against the grain of all reason and logic, and in defiance of the natural constraints of his reality, Jabez asked the Lord to change everything he was unhappy about in his life. Take a look at the words of his prayer:

> *"Oh, that You would* ***bless me*** *indeed, and* ***enlarge my territory,*** *that* ***Your hand would be with me****, and that You would* ***keep me from evil, that I may not cause pain!"***
>
> *—1 Chronicles 4:10* NKJV

Mic drop Wow.

How do you think God responded to Jabez's bold faith? Do you think He said, "Come on, Jabez, you've got to be realistic here"? No, that's what you and I might have said. But not God. **God loves bold faith.** You see, His heart is always to give, and He's just waiting to lavish His goodness on the one who simply asks of Him. What was His response to Jabez's out-of-nowhere audacious request? He granted him all that he had asked for! He even praised Jabez, calling him "more honorable" than all his brothers.

Friend, the truth of the matter is this: as therapeutic as complaining might feel, it gets you nowhere. In fact, the Hebrew word for *complain* literally means to "stay the night."[1] Now tell me, why would you want to do that? Why would you want to remain one night longer in pain, sadness, and misery?

Don't be like the people of Israel in the wilderness who were so caught up with complaining and feeling upset they couldn't see their big-hearted, miracle-working God who was all the while right there with them, waiting for them to ask of Him. Instead of getting fed up and frustrated with your situation, you can do something about it as a child of God—ask your Daddy God for the turnaround you need. He's more than willing and able to give it to you!

The next time you go through a difficult season or painful challenge, will you be like Jabez? Dare to be different, lean in to the heart of your good Father, and ask BIG!

Footnote

1. OT: 3885, James Strong, *Biblesoft's New Exhaustive Strong's Numbers and Concordance of the Bible with Expanded Greek-Hebrew Dictionary*. Copyright © 1994, 2003, 2006 Biblesoft, Inc. and International Bible Translators, Inc.

DON'T STAY ANOTHER NIGHT.

OWN THE WORD

What are some areas in your life where you find yourself repeatedly caught in a cycle of pain, frustration, or dissatisfaction? Now ask yourself, what have you been saying about these areas of your life to the people around you or to yourself?

Because complaining can be so unconscious, it would help if you were to ask a close friend about an area of your life they've noticed you complaining about and what you tend to say.

Now practice doing what Jabez did. Instead of complaining and staying one more night in that situation, ask the Lord to disrupt that cycle of defeat with His hand of blessing. Ask Him to change the situation. Ask Him to change you, if necessary. When you do, you're inviting Him—His power and His wisdom—into that area of your life to bring the turnaround you need.

READ

1 Chronicles 4:9–10

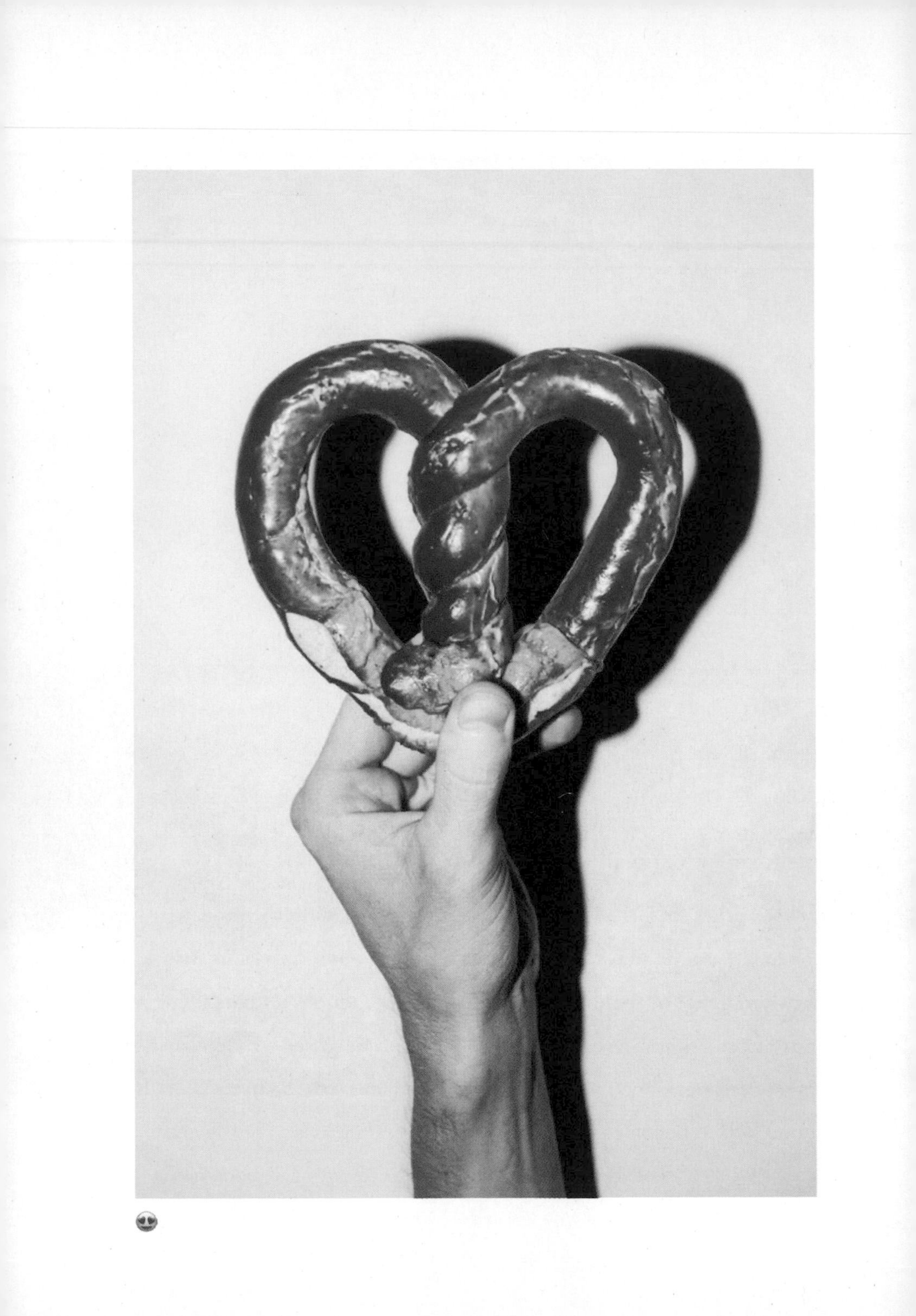

DAY SEVEN

ADDICTED TO "LIKES"

We all like to be liked. We like it when people say good things about us. We like all the 👍, 🙌, 👌, 🤩, and 🔥 that friends leave on our posts. We like it especially when these praises come from someone we want to be noticed by, like our boss, mentor, or significant other. Little else gives us the kind of kick we get from knowing we're seen, appreciated, and celebrated.

While it's great to receive affirmation and it can encourage us and spur us on in life, **our need for it becomes a problem when it pulls us into a downward spiral of feeling rejected, not good enough, and insecure about our self-worth every time it's not met.** It becomes a problem when our emotions peak and plunge based on whether or not we get a 👍 or hear a "good job!" It becomes a problem when we end up living for the gram because we're obsessed with what people think about us. It becomes a problem when we start counting and comparing the "likes" on our posts to create and curate a lifestyle based solely on what others want to see.

While being addicted to "likes" is most obvious on social media, it can permeate and affect every area of our lives.

Many of us know what it feels like to put ourselves out there—whether it's in our academic performance, careers, or our friendships and relationships—only to have our best efforts get seemingly ignored. We end up overwhelmed with self-doubt and self-consciousness, our thoughts going into overdrive, flooding our minds with fears of letting people down, worries about what they might think or say about us, and schemes of what we can do to win back their favor. Compelled by our insatiable need to be affirmed, we don our masks—playing the nice guy or girl, pretending to be funnier, smarter, more likable, more diligent—all in a bid to get our "approval fix" and feel better about ourselves.

Now here's the problem with living under the fear of people's opinions: **it's a trap.**

Proverbs 29:25 NLT tells us, "Fearing people is a dangerous trap." **Like an addiction, the craving for people's approval traps us in a place of compromise, where we will do anything to satisfy it.** So instead of being led by the voice of the Lord, the One who created us and the One whom we were created for, we end up being led by the voices of insecurity and anxiety that constantly tell us how we need to keep up appearances or, on the flip side, change the way we look, act, and speak to please others.

Did you know that there was someone in the Bible who had a hardcore addiction to "likes"? His name was Saul, better known as King Saul, the first king of Israel.

Now Saul was 100% influencer material. The Bible says this about him when he was anointed king: "There was not a more handsome person than he among the children of Israel. From his shoulders upward he was taller than any of the people" (1 Sam. 9:2 NKJV). Not only was Saul good-looking, but once he was made king, he also proved himself in numerous battles against Israel's enemies and emerged victorious, earning himself a following of loyal men. For many years, Saul ruled over Israel successfully and the people loved him.

But Saul had a problem. He wanted everyone to think he was the bomb. Everyone. Everywhere. At every moment. He wanted the approval of others so badly he began to build his life and his leadership on their opinions.

At first, this wasn't an obvious chink in his armor (an addiction to "likes" rarely is). But it became glaringly apparent when David, the new kid on the block, showed up on the scene. Saul's blood boiled when people started singing songs about how he had slain only 1,000 enemies compared to David, who had slain 10,000. This was the equivalent of people celebrating David for having 10 times more "likes" than he did! Saul got so upset, jealous, and paranoid that he made David his enemy and tried to pin him to the wall with a spear!

Envy and bitterness were the side effects of Saul's addiction to "likes." But the real problem came when Saul had to choose between what God wanted and what the people, whose "likes" he so prized, wanted.

No prizes for guessing who Saul listened to.

In 1 Samuel 15, we see how the Lord told Saul to go against the Amalekites, longtime enemies and oppressors of Israel. He promised Saul that Israel would triumph and told Saul all he had to do was *completely* destroy them and everything that belonged to them. But the people of Israel had other ideas. Saul's approval addiction kicked in and he caved, giving in to what they wanted. He kept the king of the Amalekites alive and he allowed the people to take the plunder, sheep, oxen, and the best of the things that should have been destroyed. Why? Because, as Saul himself said later on, "I feared the people and obeyed their voice" (1 Sam. 15:24 NKJV). The tragic thing is, what Saul refused to destroy, destroyed him. In the end, it was an Amalekite who killed him in battle many years later.

Now what about David, the giant slayer-turned-king whom God anointed in Saul's place?

David and Saul were actually similar in many ways. The Bible describes them both as good-looking, mighty warrior kings who were loved by the people. They were both anointed by God and had the Lord's presence with them. Yet their lives took on completely different trajectories and left vastly different legacies. Today the flag of Israel flies the Star of David while the name of Saul has gone down in infamy.

What happened?

Unlike Saul, **David lived above the trappings of man's opinion and approval of him.**

We see this most clearly in a run-in David had with the same enemy that took Saul down—the Amalekites. One day, when David and his army left their camp in Ziklag unattended, the Amalekites raided it, stealing all their belongings and capturing their wives and children. Can you see the contrast between David's situation and Saul's? While Saul was the one who attacked the Amalekites at God's command and won the battle, David was the one being attacked by the Amalekites, and it looked like he had just lost. With the grief of losing his family and the pressure of having furious men in his own army wanting to stone him, David could have easily caved and taken the path of least resistance by going along with whatever his men thought was best.

But that's not what David did.

1 Samuel 30 NKJV tells us David strengthened himself in the Lord, and then **he asked the Lord for His opinion** on whether or not they should pursue the Amalekites. It was only with the Lord's blessing that David chased down the raiders and raided them back, recovering everything he and his men had lost and gaining much more!

So what was it that made David so different from Saul? What made him immune to an addiction to "likes"?

We find the answer in 1 Chronicles 28:4 KJV where David recounts his beginnings with the Lord. He says, "Howbeit the LORD God of Israel chose me before all the house of my father to be king over Israel for ever . . . and among the sons of my father **he liked me** to make me king over all Israel."

Did you get that? David had already gotten the most important "like" from the Lord. It didn't matter to him what anyone else thought about him because he already knew what the Lord thought about him! He knew deep in his being that God didn't just love him, but He also liked him. To David, this wasn't just a nice thought. It filled his consciousness and caused him to live with a strong sense of the Lord's constant presence and delight over him. In Psalm 16:8 NASB, David talked about the unshakable security that the Lord's affirmation brought him: "I have set the LORD continually before me; because He is at my right hand, I will not be shaken."

This one "like" from the Lord would go on to define David all his life. Through all his ups and downs, whether he was at his peak of ruling over a prospering Israel or whether the nation was in disarray and rebellion, he leaned in hard on the Lord's opinion of him and depended on His guidance and voice to lead him in life. As a result, David lived a long life and "served the purpose of God in his own generation" (Acts 13:36 NASB).

Friend, that's the kind of life God wants you to live too—a life of emotional stability and security, where you're constantly affirmed and led by the One who loves you, likes you, and knows the best decisions for you to make. Like David, will you let the Lord's good opinion of you define your life and overwrite the opinions of everyone else, even your own?

Here's a simple equation for having such security in the Lord:

Security in the Lord = What the Lord says about me > what people say about me + what I think about myself

The best part about all of this is that you never have to fight or do anything to earn God's good opinion of you because you already have it. It's part of your inheritance! Ephesians 1:6 NKJV tells us that by grace we are "accepted in the Beloved." Just as Jesus was accepted and approved of by the Father before He'd even performed a single miracle in His earthly ministry, so today we are unconditionally loved and approved of even before we do anything to try to earn it. Hear your Daddy say over you today as He did over Jesus, **"You are My beloved son, in whom I am well pleased"** (Matt. 3:17 NKJV)!

This is the ultimate "like" your heavenly Father wants you to walk away with today!

OWN THE WORD

It's so important to be reminded daily of how much the Lord loves and likes you. You can set a daily reminder of Matthew 3:17, change the wallpaper on your computer or phone to reflect this message of approval, or get creative with it in your own way! We have designed some wallpapers you can use at **JosephPrince.com/gmtm**.

As you hear your heavenly Father speaking the words of Matthew 3:17 over you each day, take time to really be conscious of His delight over you. It will give you the confidence and security to go out and be the champion in life He made you to be!

READ

1 Samuel 15 / 1 Samuel 30
Matthew 3:13–17

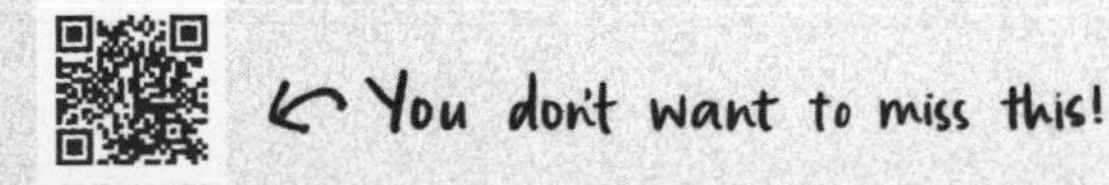

BASE CAMP 3

TAKE GROUND BY FAITH

×

LEARN HOW TO PRACTICE *WALKING BY FAITH* AND CLAIMING GOD'S PROMISES IN YOUR LIFE.

WHERE'S THE ESCALATOR?

DAY ONE

TAKE GROUND BY FAITH

See here's the thing about taking a mountain. It's rarely a brief affair. It takes more than a little effort, countless steps, and hours that can carry over into days of climbing from base to summit.

Just ask any wilderness junkie or anyone who's been on hikes or treks. More than beautiful selfies at the edge of spectacular cliffs or grand gorges, it is the journey that makes reaching the destination that much sweeter. Yes, it may involve its fair share of challenges and difficulties—navigating obstacles, enduring harsh weather and unfavorable terrain—but every step is taken with deep purpose, intentionality, and resolve that surpasses even the encumbrance of inertia, gravity, and fatigue.

Along the slopes of the mountains in our own lives, while still en route to our destination, especially when the possibility of our breakthrough seems momentarily to blip out of sight, how do we keep that same purpose and resolve to press on? How do we continue to take ground and make progress toward the dreams and promises God has placed in our hearts?

In Joshua 1:3 NKJV, God meets Joshua, the new leader of Israel, on the banks of the Jordan river as the people are making their final preparations to enter the promised land. Here, He gives Joshua a powerful insight about taking the land. He says, "**Every place that the sole of your feet will tread upon I have given you.**"

Now this statement from the Lord is an interesting one because it has a double meaning.

First, it was a personal encouragement for Joshua, reminding him that the battle was already won and the land already theirs, even though they had not yet seen it happen or made any endeavor to engage the enemy. **It was not a statement of observable fact, but a statement of believing faith.**

You see, from where the people of Israel were standing on the low-lying plains of the Jordan, they didn't have a great vantage point of the land. In fact, they couldn't see very much further than the next step they would take, which was to cross the Jordan river into the land God had for them. In other words, all they had to go on was the invisible but infallible word the Lord had given them. They had to take ground by faith!

Yet, so often along the journey of believing God, people say things out of frustration like, "If I can't see it, I won't believe it!" or "I've been believing God, so why does nothing seem to be happening?"

But friend, the very nature of faith is to believe *before* seeing.

Think about it this way. It doesn't make sense for a person to hold a cup of coffee in his hands and then confess, "I am *believing* God today for some coffee," right? He already has it! Friend, the fact of the matter is this: **the only time we can believe God or have faith is *precisely* and *only* when we don't yet see it.** It's when we don't see our breakthroughs yet still choose to trust and believe that God is faithful to make good on His promises that our faith is most alive and active!

What an encouragement to know this. That even though we might not see our miracle yet, we can still be on the right track, taking ground by faith. 2 Corinthians 5:7 NKJV succinctly summarizes our walk as believers: "we walk by faith, not by sight."

Second, the Lord's words to Joshua on the banks of the Jordan river were not only meant to assure and encourage him, but also to challenge him to *take as much of the land as he would.*

Let's think about the message the Lord gave Joshua again: "**Every place that the sole of your feet will tread upon I have given you.**" This means that if Joshua decided to walk through only half the breadth of the promised land, then that's how much of the land Israel would possess. If he decided to go into retirement early, having walked through only two-thirds of the land, then that's all the inheritance Israel would get. If he decided it was just too intimidating to even take the next step to cross the Jordan, then Israel would not possess anything at all even though the Lord had already given them the entire land!

So let me ask you this: Who determines how much you get in life today? Who decides the quality of life and fulfillment you get to enjoy? Who decides what blessings you get to experience? Who sets the limit on how much of the abundant, full-till-overflowing life you get to possess?

Many of us think it's the Lord. After all, isn't He the all-knowing Almighty God who decides all things? Yet Psalm 78:41 TPT reveals the sobering truth about who really determines how much we get in life when it describes the journey Israel took toward the promised land: "Again and again **they limited God, preventing him from blessing them.**"

That's got to be the *last thing* we want for our lives. Don't you want to know exactly what you're doing that limits God and how you can take those limits off?

The simple answer in God's Word is this: "My people are destroyed for lack of knowledge" (Hos. 4:6 NKJV). Friend, we limit the Lord by how much, or *how little*, we know about His ways of faith, who we are in Him, and the inheritance we have through Jesus' finished work at the cross. **The more we know about our inheritance and how we have access to it by faith (Rom. 4:13 NKJV), the more we will possess what's already ours!** Doesn't it behoove us then to understand all we can about this powerful thing called "faith" that God has given us?

Just like water on a hike, faith is what keeps us going on our journey toward possessing our miracles. It sustains us, it helps us see beyond the next step and obstacle, and it brings with it all of heaven's resources. In Hebrews 11, the portion of Scripture that's often referred to as the "hall of faith," we read story after story, account after account, of how men and women of God overcame impossible odds, subdued kingdoms, fought valiantly in battles, and out of weakness were made strong and obtained their breakthroughs.

And they did it all by **faith**.

This week, as we take time to dwell on powerful truths about faith, God wants to do for you what He did for them. He wants to fill your heart with fresh purpose and make you unstoppable in the face of every obstacle and plan of the enemy to discourage you. He wants to impart to you a spirit of faith and perseverance that will see you through every step of the journey. He wants to see you come out on top in every area of your life.

He wants you to take ground by **faith**.

OWN THE WORD

There's nothing like learning about the journey by actually experiencing it. Today it's time to get out of the house. Go for a run in the park, go on a hike, or take a trek in nature nearby (alternatively, if you can't get out of the house, get on YouTube and find a 30-minute home workout you don't mind trying). Take note of how you feel at the start of the journey, in the middle, and finally, at the end.

When you're done, jot down what your thoughts and feelings were throughout the activity. What made you carry on all the way till the end? Now talk to the Lord about the journeys in your life you're still taking. Tell Him how you feel about them and ask Him to teach you more about His ways of faith.

READ

Joshua 1 / Hosea 4:6
Romans 4:13 / Hebrews 11:4–39

3-SHELL MONTE.

DAY TWO

FAITH IS *NOT* A FEELING

If you've ever had a go at a game of 3-shell monte, *you've probably been played.*

What's 3-shell monte? Well here's typically how it goes: A single ball is placed under one of 3 identical cups or "shells" that are then shuffled in quick succession by the dealer in plain view. After this shuffling, the player is asked to point out which shell the ball is under. If he gets it right, he wins. If he doesn't, the dealer takes his money.

Sounds simple enough, right? Well, yes, if it was played fairly. In practice, the game is notorious for being used by confidence tricksters who, through deft sleight of hand, switch and hide the ball during play, misleading the player and then placing the ball conveniently where required. For the poor unsuspecting player who doesn't know any better, it is a perfect con job.

Now you might be wondering, *Why are we talking about 3-shell monte, and what does it have to do with me understanding faith?*

Here's why.

The enemy is a wily one. The Bible calls him a thief, a liar, and a snake, whose singular agenda is to steal, kill, and destroy (John 10:10 NKJV). And when it comes to faith, perhaps the biggest con job he's pulled on believers who don't know better is this: **he swaps out our *faith* and substitutes it with our *feelings*.**

Just think about all the thoughts and feelings that so often stop us in our tracks every time we try to take ground by faith, like:

I just feel like I don't have enough faith.

I've tried believing God but I don't feel like it's working!

That thing I'm hoping for is not logically possible given the circumstances.

I messed up. I don't think God's going to answer me.

I don't know if I really believe . . . I'm just not feeling it.

Like a crafty dealer in a game of 3-shell monte, he draws your eye away from the sure and unshakable foundation for your faith—the Word of God—and instead gets you to focus on how you *feel* based on how things look in your situation. You step out of church full of faith on Sunday, but before you know it, you find yourself deflated and demoralized come Monday.

What just happened? You've been played!

My friend, enough is enough! It's time to call the devil out on his ruse!

Faith is NOT a feeling.

Our feelings are subject to the ebb and flow of our daily experiences. Can you imagine what it would be like if our faith were really predicated on our feelings? Depending on whether we're having a good day or woke up on the wrong side of bed, depending on whether we mess up that day or not, our faith would follow our feelings on all their ups and downs. Is that the sort of faith God meant for us to have? No way.

So if faith is not a feeling, then what is it?

In Hebrews 11:1 NKJV, God gives us this definition of faith: "Faith is the **substance** of things hoped for, the **evidence** of things not seen." Notice the Lord's deliberate choice of words to describe the faith we are to have. He uses words like *substance* and *evidence* that convey a sense of tangible, concrete, and almost indisputable surety. This tells us that although faith is unseen, it is not airy or flaky. It is certain, secure, and sure!

Do you know why? Because it is based on the unshakable Word of God that speaks of the irreversible work of Jesus at the cross. That's why the Bible tells us that **faith comes by hearing the good news about Christ** (Rom. 10:17 NLT)!

So what is faith? Faith is a spiritual **decision** to believe in the Lord, His Word, and His work for us. It's a decision that's borne out of an intimate relationship with the person of Jesus and sustained by Him.

Now does that mean our feelings and emotions don't matter? Does it mean we should never feel scared or worried again? Of course not. But what it does mean is that our faith is **separate** from our feelings.

FAITH | FEELINGS

Because they are separate, it means that **even though you have feelings, they don't have to affect your faith!** Just look at these characters in the Bible who, in spite of the adversities they faced and how they felt, held fast to their faith and saw their breakthroughs!

- **David** at Ziklag, at one of the lowest points in his life after his enemies had plundered his city and home, encouraged himself in the Lord (1 Sam. 30 KJV).

- **Jehoshaphat**, in fear when 3 heathen armies beyond number had gathered themselves against him, set himself to seek the Lord (2 Chron. 20:1–30 NKJV).

- **Jeremiah**, afraid to face the people God had called him to speak to, received a revelation from God and showed up to preach anyway (Jer. 1:1–10 NKJV).

Isn't that freeing to know? That it's okay to feel the way you do and not let it affect your faith? And that's not all. Not only is faith separate from your feelings, but it is also **superior** to your feelings.

FAITH

FEELINGS

That simply means that what you believe has the power to affect how you feel! We don't need feelings to validate our faith, but when we believe right about the Lord, our right believing produces the right feelings.

In Psalm 56:11 NKJV, the writer pens these powerful words about faith in the Lord: "In God I have put my trust; I will not be afraid." We see here that choosing to trust the Lord results in fear being driven from our hearts. Choosing to declare His Word by faith exerts a positive influence on our emotions.

Friend, there's nothing wrong with having feelings, but God doesn't want your feelings to rule over your life. He wants the reality of His abundant grace and the unbreakable relationship you have with Him to dominate your heart and mind so that you will reign over every area of life—even in your feelings and emotions (Rom. 5:17 NKJV)!

So now you know better. Next time someone tries to pull a fast one on you and get you to examine how you feel to determine whether you're in faith or not, don't fall for it!

OWN THE WORD

Take authority over how you have been feeling this past week. Begin by finding passages of Scripture that speak life into the situations you are facing (you can use those from the readings below) and confess them out loud. Don't focus on how you feel as you do it. Simply declare and speak out God's words of truth by faith! You'll realize the powerful effect of your words over how you feel once you start declaring the Word by faith.

READ

Hebrews 11:1–2 / 1 Samuel 30

2 Chronicles 20:1–30 / Jeremiah 1:1–10

← There's more to learn here.

bae today was lit 🔥🔥 saw these new pair of kicks at the store 🙏🙏 on fleek 🙏🙏 so gonna get em 👟👟👟

4:07 PM

👍👍🖤

4:07 PM ✓✓

DAY THREE

GOD SLANG

YOLO. *FOMO*. That's so *lit*. Outfit *on fleek*. I'm *shook*. Stay *woke*. You *slay*. *Yeet*!

Every generation has its own slang.

Just mention some of these words to a person and the look of either utter confusion or immediate understanding on their face will locate exactly which generation they're part of, whether Gen X, Millennial, or Gen Z.

What is slang? It's an informal collection of words and phrases, more common in speech than in writing, used among people within a certain group or context. It's a way of speaking that bonds people together. It creates a shared sense of identity, synergy, and solidarity.

Did you know that God has slang too? He has a way of speaking for His people to latch on to that will cause them to walk in their identity as His sons and daughters and experience the power and results His words produce.

In Mark 11:12–14, 20–22 NKJV, Jesus demonstrated the power of this divine pattern of speech when He cursed a fig tree for not bearing fruit. The next day, as He and His disciples passed by the same way, the disciples were flabbergasted to find the fig tree had shriveled up and withered. They gathered around their Master, amazed and eager to learn more about how something like that could happen. Jesus' reply? "Have faith of God" (Mark 11:22 YLT) or "**Have God's faith.**" Notice how Jesus didn't rebuke them for asking. Instead, He invited them to partake of this same power and ability He and His Father shared—the power of God slang.

This slang and way of speaking is called **faith**! And today, He is extending that same invitation to you. When you learn God's language of faith, you will see and experience God-kind of results.

How many of us are glad Jesus didn't just stop there? The author of faith Himself continued to teach them about this wonderful language of faith. Jesus followed up by saying:

> *"For assuredly, I say to you, whoever* **says** *to this mountain, 'Be removed and be cast into the sea,' and does not doubt in his heart, but believes that those things he* **says** *will be done, he will have whatever he* **says**."
>
> *—Mark 11:23–24* NKJV

Did you get that? Look at just how many times Jesus mentions the word *says*. Friend, what God wants you to know about how the language of faith works is that **faith speaks**. The way that you exercise your blood-bought authority as a believer in the face of every mountain in your life—the challenge you are facing, the obstacle in your way—is to simply believe and then speak! In Romans 10:10 NKJV, the voice of the risen Christ through the apostle Paul further ratifies this by telling us, "For with the heart one believes unto righteousness, and **with the mouth confession is made unto salvation.**" The word *salvation* here comes from the Greek word *sōzō*, which actually refers to being saved from all kinds of peril in life, to be set free, to be restored, to be made whole, to be healed![1]

Wow, that's a mouthful. But what this verse simply means is that by the same way we received the greatest gift—salvation through Jesus Christ—we also receive every other accompanying gift and blessing into our lives—by speaking! By speaking out in faith, we can move *even* mountains.

Jesus then went deeper still in His explanation of the language of faith.

He told His disciples that whatever things they spoke or asked for in prayer, they had to **believe that they had already received them before actually having them** (Mark 11:24 NKJV). This is exactly what He demonstrated with the fig tree. He didn't speak the words, "Let no one eat fruit from you ever again," then grab a stool, sit down beside the tree, and wonder to Himself, "Hmm . . . I wonder what's taking so long." No. The moment Jesus spoke, He believed what He had spoken to the tree had already taken place at its roots. He didn't need to see it happen to believe that the miracle had taken place! To the Lord, it was as if it had *already happened*.

What He was asking His disciples to do was to believe without seeing and then **start acting as if what they had asked for had already happened.** This probably reminded His disciples of something else He had told them in an earlier encounter, where He had encouraged them to respond to the promises in God's Word by believing and speaking as if they had already received what those promises said they had. He told them, "For whoever **has**, to him more will be given; but whoever does not have, even what he has will be taken away from him" (Mark 4:25 NKJV). The word *has* in the original Greek language means "to own" or "to possess."[2] How do we own our miracle? By claiming it with our words—speaking it out!

So there are two things the Lord wants us to get about the language of faith. First, **faith is a deep revelation that we already have what we ask for in prayer.** It is the divine realization and belief that we have *all* that God's Word says we have even before reality proves it!

Second, the Lord is encouraging us to **speak and act as if it's been done**, as if we already have our miracle. When you start saying by faith, "I have it!" God says, "Yes, you do! And you shall have!" Because the truth is that you *really* do have it. Every spiritual blessing has already been made available to us in Christ. Not being able to see it yet does not make it any less real.

SPEAK HEAVEN'S WAY.

In fact, in biblical Hebrew, there is no future tense.[3] It's almost as if God designed the language of His people in such a way that they would always speak as though they already possessed all the good things they spoke of! For example, when we read the blessings in Deuteronomy 28 in our English Bibles, they all seem to start out with, "Blessed *shall you be*," implying the blessing had not come to pass yet. But the word *shall* was added by translators for readability, meaning it isn't there in the original Hebrew text. It would be more accurate to read it then as, "Blessed *are you already*"!

Romans 4:17 NKJV summarizes the very nature of God slang this way: **He "calls those things that do not exist as though they did."** Friend, this is the way God speaks. He doesn't speak what He sees. He always speaks what He *wants* to see!

I know this goes against everything we're used to. Are we really supposed to look at the very real and visible mountain looming before us and offer invisible confessions and words? Can our speech really change the hopeless situation in front of us when even our best efforts can't?

The disciples, obviously feeling the same way about the inadequacy of their faith and their words, asked Jesus this: "Lord, increase our faith!" To which Jesus answered, "If you have faith as a mustard seed, you can say to this mulberry tree, 'Be pulled up by the roots and be planted in the sea,' and it would obey you" (Luke 17:5–6 NKJV).

Have you ever seen a mustard seed? It's among the smallest of all seeds. Some are not much bigger than the period at the end of this sentence. It's so tiny and near invisible that you'd probably miss it if you weren't looking out for it. Doesn't that remind us of how we feel about the impact of our words? What Jesus was telling them was that **while our words of faith might seem as small, invisible, and insignificant as a mustard seed, they have the power to uproot something as massive as a tree!**

Just as God beheld the darkness and the void at the dawn of creation and said, "Let there be light!", and light was; just as Jesus in a storm-swept fishing boat on the Sea of Galilee looked the tempest square in the eye and declared to it the peace He wanted to see, God wants us to pick up His slang today and speak forth what we *want to see*.

2 Corinthians 4:13 TPT tells us, "We have the same Spirit of faith that is described in the Scriptures when it says, 'First I believed, then I spoke in faith.' So we also first believe then speak in faith." It's as simple as that. We believe, we speak, and power is released to change what we're seeing into what we want to see. The Lord wants us to know His words in our mouths are as powerful as His words in His mouth!

Do you want to see results? Do you want to see your mountains move?

Then start speaking God slang today!

OWN THE WORD

Like all slangs, God slang is not meant to be spoken only to yourself. So find someone to practice it with! Call or text a friend to hang out, then try this activity together: take turns to declare God's promises and blessings over each other.

Remember that when it comes to God slang, it's all about speaking forth what God sees, not what you see in the natural. You can prepare some verses you want to speak over your friend beforehand, and you can also listen and give voice to all the good things the Lord tells you on the spot about them (their life, their future, etc.). In keeping with how biblical Hebrew has no future tense, speak God's blessings over your friend as though they've already come to pass!

Lastly, respond to each other's good declarations by believing and receiving each one with an "amen!" In Hebrew, that means "truly" or "so be it"[4]—a powerful term in God slang too.

READ

Deuteronomy 28:1–13 / Mark 11:23–24
Luke 17:5–6

Footnotes

1. NT: 4982, James Strong, *Biblesoft's New Exhaustive Strong's Numbers and Concordance of the Bible with Expanded Greek-Hebrew Dictionary*. Copyright © 1994, 2003, 2006 Biblesoft, Inc. and International Bible Translators, Inc.
2. NT: 2192, James Strong, *Biblesoft's New Exhaustive Strong's Numbers and Concordance of the Bible with Expanded Greek-Hebrew Dictionary*. Copyright © 1994, 2003, 2006 Biblesoft, Inc. and International Bible Translators, Inc.
3. Young, Robert. "Young's Literal Translation of the Holy Bible." Young's Translation: Publisher's Note & Preface (1898). Christian Classics Ethereal Library. Accessed April 14, 2020. https://www.ccel.org/bible/ylt/ylt.htm.
4. NT: 281, James Strong, *Biblesoft's New Exhaustive Strong's Numbers and Concordance of the Bible with Expanded Greek-Hebrew Dictionary*. Copyright © 1994, 2003, 2006 Biblesoft, Inc. and International Bible Translators, Inc.

ADULTING BE LIKE . . .

DAY FOUR

THE FAITH FOR EVERYTHING

Ever felt like you had to grow up way faster than you thought? Suddenly and without warning, you were launched into a whole new world of adulting that nothing could have prepared you for. Housing, rent, student loan debt, career choices, life-partner decisions . . . With so many real responsibilities to deal with, you've never had more things to worry about and use your faith for.

But let me ask you this: **If you could use your faith for just *one thing*, what would it be?**

Take a moment to think about it. Would it be for that breakthrough in your finances? Would it be for that recommendation letter or that job promotion? Would it be for answers to all your questions about your love life? Or maybe you can't decide because there are just too many spaces in your life where you need God to come through for you.

Friend, get this: above all else, God wants you to use your faith for righteousness.

When Jesus was on earth, He saw the overwhelming need people had for His provision in their lives. And He saw that they were stressed out and worried sick about trying to get it. His heart swelled with compassion for them, and He told them, "Do not worry, saying, 'What shall we eat?' or 'What shall we drink?' or 'What shall we wear?' For after all these things the [unbelievers] seek. For your heavenly Father knows that you need all these things. But **seek first the kingdom of God and His righteousness, and all these things shall be added to you**" (Matt. 6:31–33 NKJV).

Notice how Jesus is telling us to seek first *His* righteousness, not ours? Not our fragile righteousness based on our inconsistent behavior but His perfect righteousness. He's saying that when we use our faith to believe that we have received His righteousness, we will receive every blessing and breakthrough we need.

Now you might be thinking, *That sounds very spiritual but not very practical.*

Friend, if there's one thing that stops us from receiving from God, one thing that stops us from daring to pray and ask God for what we need, it's that nagging feeling of guilt or shame whenever we mess up. Which, if we're honest, is daily.

Think about it. When you're feeling guilty because you've failed in some way, are you going to happily run to God to ask Him for favors? No way. Instead, you'll wonder, *How can I go to God? I don't deserve His favor, His goodness, His help. He might be my Dad and all but He's probably still low-key mad at me for what I did.* And so we run *from* God instead of run *to* Him. We might still go to church on Sundays and do all the outwardly "Christian" things, but in our hearts, we feel miles away from God. That's what condemnation does to us.

And that's why above all else, Jesus wants us to use our faith for righteousness. He wants us to use our faith to believe that at the cross, He really took every last one of our sins—past, present, and even future—and gave us *His* righteousness (2 Cor. 5:21 NKJV). This also means that when God looks at us today, He sees us as sinless and faultless as Jesus is because we are in Christ.

This changes everything, doesn't it? Now we can freely run to our Father any time, any day, knowing He's welcoming us with open arms. It gives us the assurance that we never have to earn His blessings because "blessings are on the head of the righteous" (Prov. 10:6 NKJV). It gives us the confidence to ask Him for big things, knowing there's nothing stopping Him from giving and nothing stopping us from receiving!

So when it comes to:

Your thought life

Negative, self-condemning, self-loathing thoughts do not have a place in your life when you believe that you are dressed in Jesus' righteousness. God has "brought you into his own presence, and you are holy and blameless as you stand before him without a single fault" (Col. 1:22 NLT).

Your health

You can be sure that God's not punishing you with sickness or withholding healing from you because of something wrong you did in the past. Psalm 103:3 NLT says, "He forgives all my sins and heals all my diseases." Because you have Jesus' righteousness, you can receive your healing and restoration for any area you need, body or mind.

Your finances

Settling your debts, paying the rent, planning for the future, and have no idea where the money you need is going to come from? Friend, even if you made mistakes or unwise choices that have led you to where you are at this point, know that God has already put those sins on Jesus and put Jesus' righteousness on you. Today you can believe for provision, supernatural debt cancellation, and wisdom to manage and multiply your money (Deut. 8:18 NKJV).

Your love life

If you've failed in relationships time and time again and feel like there's something wrong with you, the Lord wants you to know that because you have His righteousness, today is a new day. You can ask Him to break any toxic cycle you've been stuck in and do a new thing in your life. Let Him paint you a picture of the beautiful, healthy, better-than-any-thing-you've-ever-experienced kind of relationship He wants you to enjoy, and let Him lead you into it step by step!

Your studies or career

You can replace every fear, self-condemning thought, or negative label that's been put on you—that you're a bad student, lousy employee, useless worker—with this truth: *I am the righteousness of God in Christ.* When you start believing that you have Jesus' righteousness on you, the Lord will bring you from the bottom to the top and "make you the head and not the tail" (Deut. 28:13 NKJV)!

Friend, this is why Proverbs 21:21 TPT says, "**The lovers of God who chase after righteousness will find all their dreams come true**: an abundant life drenched with favor and a fountain that overflows with satisfaction." Use your faith for righteousness and all these things will be added to you!

OWN THE WORD

Take time to run through, again, the different areas of life and adulting highlighted at the end of today's teaching, and journal down any worries or fears you might have in those areas. Then read Matthew 6:31–33 and listen to what the Lord has to say to you and encourage you with.

READ

Matthew 6:31–33 / 2 Corinthians 5:21

← That's not all! Watch this!

TUG-O-BREAD.

DAY FIVE

FIGHTING = FEEDING

Has life ever taken a swing at you so hard it knocked you completely off balance? That swing might be getting a bad report about the health of a loved one. It might be experiencing a betrayal by a family member or someone close to you. Or it might be a sudden turn of events for the worst . . . *just* when you thought you were making progress.

For some of us, our instinctive response when adversity hits us is to tense up, grit our teeth, and get ready to fight our way through whatever comes, often with great casualty to our hearts or to those closest to us. Then there are those of us who immediately duck for cover and get on the first train out to *Runaway-ville*, choosing to selectively and completely tune out the pain and bury the way we feel.

When life hits you hard like a punch in the gut, what is your response? To fight? Or to take flight? **More importantly, what is God's best for us when this happens?**

Let's take a look at a story in Exodus 17:8–13 NKJV, where life in the form of the Amalekites came looking to pick a fight with God's people. Threatened by the Israelites fresh out of slavery in Egypt, the Amalekites attacked them as they camped at Rephidim, a place where its name actually means "resting places."[1] My friend, there are no insignificant details in the Bible. God wants you to know the tactic and agenda of the enemy: **the devil wants to disrupt your rest as a believer.** He wants you stressed out, losing sleep, feeling like it all depends on you to deal with the problem in front of you. He wants to make you feel like you need to fight to keep the promises that Jesus through His sacrifice already paid for you to have. Most insidious of all, he wants you to labor and toil with your own painful efforts, as if what Jesus did at Calvary was not enough. In fact, that is exactly what the root word of *Amalekites* means in Hebrew: "painful toil."[2]

Guess what brilliant military strategy Moses, the leader of Israel, came up with in response to this challenge by the Amalekites? He told Joshua, his right-hand man, to take some men and go down to fight them, while he went up to the top of a nearby hill, sat down on a rock, and held up the rod of God.

Some of you might be wondering at this point, *Wait a minute, is that responsible leadership? Leaving your men to head into battle while you take a back seat?*

But what happened next is nothing short of extraordinary: As long as Moses held up the rod of God, Israel prevailed. But when he was tired and put it down, Amalek prevailed. It didn't seem to matter what Joshua did or how skillful the men he had with him were. All that mattered was whether Moses had his arms raised! When the 2 men who accompanied Moses realized this, they immediately stood next to him, one on each side, supporting his arms so they would remain perpetually raised.

Now imagine this with me: We have a time machine and we travel back in time to this exact moment in the story to help with the outcome of the battle. To that very fork in the road, with one path leading down to the battle and the other leading up to the top of the hill. What would you do? Which path would you take? Where would you go to make a real difference?

Without a doubt and with the benefit of hindsight, most of us would, in a heartbeat, choose to head up the hill! That's good and fantastic in our hypothetical illustration, but where the rubber meets the road is in our own lives. When the enemy throws a fight in our direction, what do we do? If we're honest, so many times we respond by running hastily down to the battle, desperate to hold things together or to salvage what we can, instead of simply lifting up the rod of God, which is a picture of the cross of Jesus, our ultimate victory.

Friend, the devil wants us in a posture of stressful, toilsome labor, but **God wants us to adopt a posture of rest in faith that every promise is ours because of Jesus.** Hebrews 10:12 NKJV tells us this: "But this Man, after He had offered one sacrifice for sins forever, sat down at the right hand of God." The reason we can sit down today is that we are in Christ, seated with Him because of His finished work (Eph. 2:6 NKJV).

Does that mean we do absolutely nothing? Not at all. Hebrews 4:11 NIV says, "Let us, therefore, **make every effort** to enter that rest."

Why? Because it's completely counterintuitive to our fleshly nature to rest! It sounds unrealistic and ridiculous to our logical minds and upbringing where so many times we're told that if we don't get up and do something about it, nothing will get done! If there's any fight for a believer today, it is this: fight to come to rest. It takes real faith to look your challenge in the eye, and then sit down, lean back, and trust that the Lord has taken care of it.

Faith is all about resting.

When we rest, God's grace, His unmerited favor, goes to work in our situations. When we rest, God fights on our behalf. And the great thing about the Lord fighting our battles is that unlike us, He *doesn't* get weary, He *doesn't* make mistakes, and He *doesn't* lose.

Remember what we talked about in Week 1 about rest? It is not inactivity, but Jesus-directed activity. As you adopt a posture of resting in Him, you will experience Him leading you. For example, God's Spirit of grace can direct you to do the right thing at the right time—at work, in school, in your relationships—resulting in the best outcomes. He will open doors of opportunity for you that you can't open on your own and lead you into

TAKE A LOVE BREAK.

them step by step. A clear sign that you're in a posture of rest is that you're led by God's Spirit of grace straight into your breakthroughs minus the stress and anxiety that usually get to you!

Now are you ready to give the devil a black eye? Look at this powerful secret God has hidden for us in Psalm 23:5 NLT: **"You prepare a feast for me in the presence of my enemies."** In the midst of the unfavorable circumstances and situations we face, God has prepared a feast for us. He wants us to sit down and feed, not fight! In fact, the Hebrew letters that spell the word *feed* (*lechem*) also spell the word *fight* (*lacham*)![3]

What is God trying to tell us here? Simply this: **when you feed on His love for you through His Word, you are actually fighting back** against all that the enemy is doing. Friend, feed on scriptures that warm your heart with the tenderness of Jesus toward you. Feed on messages that deepen your understanding of His grace and His finished work. Feed on devotionals that remind you of what He's accomplished for you at the cross. In fact, that's what you're doing right now! And the more you stay in this wonderful posture of rest, taking time to strengthen and nourish yourself with God's Word, the more you'll see the Lord's grace work in your life.

I want to share with you a short testimony from Sarah, a student who saw a 180-degree turnaround in her grades when she simply fed on what Jesus had done for her at the cross.

Sarah hadn't been doing well in school. In her mid-year exams, she flunked three of her core subjects. So this is what her parents did: they started playing my sermons in their home and car as often as they could when she was around. It wasn't immediate but as Sarah listened repeatedly to the messages, things started to change. She started to place her hope and reliance on the Lord and her attitude toward her studies improved dramatically. Soon peace and rest began to replace the stress of school. 6 months later, in her final-year examination, Sarah couldn't believe her grades for the core subjects that she had failed half a year ago. She did so well she received 2 awards: one for being among the top students in class and another for having made the best progress!

Friend, this is an example of how God's grace can work for you when you feed on His Word and rest, not fight. He brings your wins to you!

Footnotes

1. OT: 7508, James Strong, *Biblesoft's New Exhaustive Strong's Numbers and Concordance of the Bible with Expanded Greek-Hebrew Dictionary*. Copyright © 1994, 2003, 2006 Biblesoft, Inc. and International Bible Translators, Inc.
2. OT: 5998, James Strong, *Biblesoft's New Exhaustive Strong's Numbers and Concordance of the Bible with Expanded Greek-Hebrew Dictionary*. Copyright © 1994, 2003, 2006 Biblesoft, Inc. and International Bible Translators, Inc.
3. OT: 3899, James Strong, *Biblesoft's New Exhaustive Strong's Numbers and Concordance of the Bible with Expanded Greek-Hebrew Dictionary*. Copyright © 1994, 2003, 2006 Biblesoft, Inc. and International Bible Translators, Inc.; OT: 3898, James Strong, *Biblesoft's New Exhaustive Strong's Numbers and Concordance of the Bible with Expanded Greek-Hebrew Dictionary*. Copyright © 1994, 2003, 2006 Biblesoft, Inc. and International Bible Translators, Inc.

OWN THE WORD

Think about a challenge you're currently facing or struggling with. It could be something less than ideal happening in the area of your family, friendships, studies, or career. What was your first response? Did you resort to your own strength, effort, or smarts to try to solve the problem?

Whatever your response, take time to talk to the Lord and commit it to Him in prayer. Ask Him to lead you and guide you as to what path to take (Prov. 3:5–6 NLT).

Now spend some time in His Word and get some good preaching to feed on!

READ

Exodus 17:8–13 / Hebrews 4:11
Hebrews 10:12

ALL FOR ONE, ONE FOR ALL.

DAY SIX

UNSTOPPABLE ALLIANCES: CALEB & JOSHUA

We've all heard the saying, "Two heads are better than one."

This is especially true when it comes to sports. In a sport like basketball, it's near-impossible for any one player to single-handedly bear the weight of the team and carry them to victory. That's why having a partner is so important.

Think about the great duos down through basketball's hall of fame: greats like Stephen Curry and Klay Thompson, LeBron James and Dwayne Wade, Shaq and Kobe, or Jordan and Bugs Bunny (just kidding)!

In terms of their skills on the court, preferred playing positions, and even personalities and temperaments, some of these players could not be more different from each other.

Yet beyond their differences as individuals, there was just something about their partnership—the chemistry and synergy it produced—that propelled their teams into winning streaks, playoff runs, and even championship wins. Every time these pairs hit the court, they were unstoppable.

The Bible, too, is not short on such unstoppable alliances.

There was Moses and Aaron, Daniel and his friends, David and Jonathan, and of course, Caleb and Joshua! All men of God who by faith in Him carried out mighty exploits: delivered their nation, slayed giants, conquered armies, and fulfilled their calls. And they did so while spurred on by their relationships with one another.

Now they too had their differences but they had one thing that bound them together. **It was the power of their agreement.**

Amos 3:3 NKJV tells us that in order for two people to walk or journey together, they first need to be able to agree. Their agreement forms the basis of shared values and beliefs, from which they have a common understanding of how to make decisions and take action. Deep and strong agreement produces powerful and synergistic relationships.

Caleb and Joshua shared such a relationship. Both part of the initial 12 spies sent to scout out the land, they found themselves on the same side—standing against the other 10—resolute in their belief that God would give them the land.

What did they agree on? **The way they saw the Lord.** They saw that He was faithful and trustworthy. They saw that He was on their side. They saw that He had a portion for each of them.

And the result of their powerful agreement was that they saw themselves well able to possess the land. They saw themselves as giant killers instead of grasshoppers! This alliance would see them through 40 years in the wilderness and prove instrumental in them leading the new generation of Israelites into the promised land.

Ecclesiastes 4:9–10 NLT gives us an insightful picture of a relationship that Joshua and Caleb might have shared: "**Two people are better off than one**, for they can help each other succeed. If one person falls, the other can reach out and help."

Unlike in basketball, our lives have far more at stake than a stellar season or a championship trophy. You can't afford not having people and friends around you who share the same beliefs and faith in a good God who loves you and is for you.

My friend, God's desire for you today is that you too might have godly alliances with like-minded people around you!

He wants you to have friends whom you can pour out your heart to and be encouraged by. Friends who will not just echo what the culture today or your situation is saying, but who will speak God's words to you and remind you of how faithful He is. Friends who can pray and believe with you for the turnarounds and breakthroughs you want to see in your life. Friends who will spur you on in the destiny and plan God has for you.

These unstoppable alliances will **allow the Lord to strengthen you, strengthen others through you**, and keep you on track to take your mountain!

1:1,000. 2:10,000.

OWN THE WORD

You're not meant to take this journey of faith alone.

If you've been going to church on Sundays and leaving once the service ends, or if you've been volunteering in church but hardly ever find the time to sit down with someone and have a real conversation with them about the journey of faith you're on, can I encourage you to open your life to someone you trust in your church community?

If you've already done so, why not look around you and reach out to someone who hasn't? Ask the Lord to show you the person(s) He wants you to reach out to and take that first step to be a friend to him or her.

You can form powerful unstoppable alliances today!

READ

Amos 3:3 / Ecclesiastes 4:9–10

← You don't want to miss this!

"SO TELL ME . . . WHAT'S YOUR SECRET?"

DAY SEVEN

CALEB'S ULTIMATE SECRET

Indomitable. Fearless. Decisive. Full of *chutzpah*.

These are just some of the words that come to mind when we think about the kind of man and leader Caleb was. From the Scriptures, we can see he was a man full of faith with steely, unshakable confidence in the Lord matched only by his fierce tenacity and relentless zeal to possess all that the Lord had given him.

So what better way to close this week of learning about God's ways of faith than to deep dive into Caleb's ultimate secret? After all, this is the guy who held on to God's promise for 45 years. This is the guy whose faith, hope, and strength never waned through all that time in the wilderness. This is that guy who, at 85 years old, took out giants and took the mountain God had promised him in his youth.

So imagine if we could sit down and have a no-holds-barred interview with the man himself, and ask him this question: *Caleb, what's the ultimate secret to having faith like yours?*

Joshua 14:7–8 NLT gives us an idea of what he might say:

> *"I was forty years old when Moses, the servant of the LORD, sent me from Kadesh-barnea to explore the land of Canaan. I returned and gave an* **honest report***, but my brothers who went with me frightened the people from entering the Promised Land.* ***For my part, I wholeheartedly followed the LORD my God."***

Did you get that? To Caleb, **his faith was simply a result of him following the Lord.** In fact, it's almost as if he was oblivious to the spirit of faith he carried. To Caleb, all he did was give an honest report of what he saw and what he believed about the God he knew. If we were to ask him how he would describe himself, his answer would very likely be, "Honestly, I'm just a guy who follows the Lord."

It seems as though the spirit of faith we so admire and esteem in Caleb was to him nothing more than a by-product of his intimate walk with the Lord. Did you notice the little word Caleb used to describe the Lord? He referred to Him as "the LORD **my** God." This small word, so easily overlooked, reveals to us how close and personal Caleb's relationship with the Lord was. It was this relationship that defined his perspective and ignited his faith.

While the Bible in its original Hebrew text doesn't record Caleb as having "faith," it records 3 times that he "**wholeheartedly followed the Lord.**" The first time was by Caleb's own admission (Josh. 14:8 NLT). The second time was by his leader, Moses, who affirmed him for it (Josh. 14:9 NLT). And the third time was by God Himself, who attested to the "different spirit" Caleb had in following Him (Num. 14:24 MSG).

So if Caleb's unstoppable faith was the outcome of simply following the Lord, how do we do that? How do we go about following Jesus in the face of life's challenges, obstacles, and mountains filled with giants? Sounds like quite a feat, right?

To answer that, we're going forward 1,500 years to look at the life of a man who had this same spirit of following the Lord. He was the apostle John. John followed Jesus from the start of His earthly ministry and was right beside Him to witness every miracle He performed. Not only did John follow Jesus during His life, but he also followed Jesus all the way to His death. When the rest of the disciples had deserted Jesus, John alone stood at the foot of the cross, still wholly following his Lord to the very end.

Now if we were to interview John and ask him what his secret to following the Lord was, what do you think he would say?

Very likely, this: "Honestly, I don't try very hard to follow Jesus. I just know that I'm **the disciple whom Jesus loved.**"

For real?

Yes! We know this because John affectionately refers to himself with these very words, *the disciple whom Jesus loved*, 5 times in his own gospel (John 13:23; 19:26; 20:2; 21:7; 21:20 NKJV). I want to draw your attention to the last time he uses this phrase to describe himself:

> *"[Jesus] said to [Peter], "Follow Me." Then Peter, turning around, saw* **the disciple whom Jesus loved following."**
> *—John 21:19–20* NKJV

Do you see how John didn't need to be told to follow the Lord? He was *already* following Him! Because John was so conscious of Jesus' love for him, following Jesus was only natural. It was unconscious and effortless.

Now was John really the Lord's favorite among the 12 disciples? Or was he just more conscious of the Lord's love for him than the rest? I would argue it's the latter because the phrase *the disciple whom Jesus loved* appears only in John's own gospel—nowhere else! It's clear John had a deep and personal revelation that **the Lord really loved him**. He didn't just *know* it, but he *believed* it and was always conscious of that love.

John and Caleb were two special people in the Bible who followed Jesus from their youth till old age—regardless of situations that seemed to contradict the Lord's goodness and power working in their lives. And they shared this same secret: they knew in the deepest parts of their beings that ***the Lord loved them.*** When they couldn't be sure of anything else, when

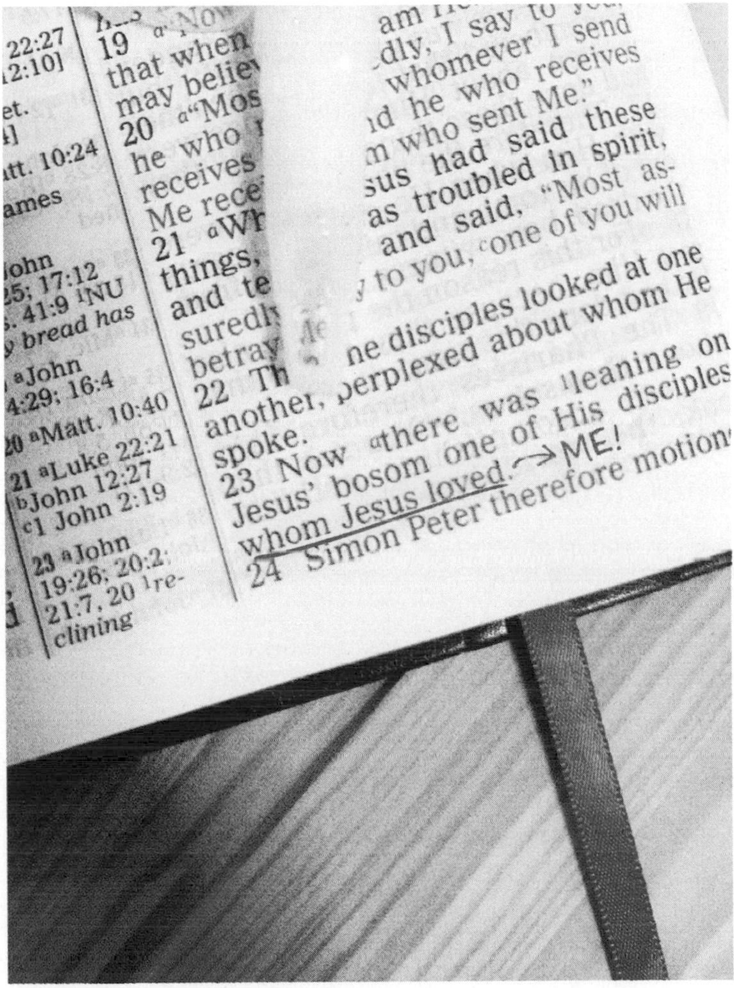

22:27
12:10]
et.
tt. 10:24
ames
John
25; 17:12
s. 41:9 1NU
y bread has
aJohn
4:29; 16:4
20 aMatt. 10:40
21 aLuke 22:21
bJohn 12:27
c1 John 2:19
23 aJohn
19:26; 20:2;
21:7, 20 1re-
clining

19 a"Now
that when
may belie
20 a"Mos
he who
receives
Me rece
21 aWh
things,
and te
suredly
betray
22 Th
am I
dly, I say to you
whomever I send
d he who receives
n who sent Me."
sus had said these
as troubled in spirit,
and said, "Most as-
y to you, cone of you will
ne disciples looked at one
another, perplexed about whom He
spoke.
23 Now athere was 1leaning on
Jesus' bosom one of His disciples
whom Jesus loved. → ME!
24 Simon Peter therefore motion

PERSONALIZE HIS LOVE FOR YOU.

everything around them seemed to be falling apart, their faith never failed because it was fueled by the Lord's unfailing love for them!

I love how the most profound secrets are hidden in the most simple truths. Most of us are familiar with the beautiful hymn "Jesus Loves Me" composed by William Bradbury in 1862 with the added simple yet powerful refrain:

> *Yes, Jesus loves me!*
> *Yes, Jesus loves me!*
> *Yes, Jesus loves me!*
> *For the Bible tells me so.*

Some people discount this hymn as a children's song or as the mere basics of Christianity, but the truth is that the revelation that *Jesus loves* ***you*** is the be-all and end-all of being a follower of Christ. It is the key to being a believing believer—one whose faith is anchored in the faithfulness and reliability of God and His Word as opposed to one who can only believe God on good days.

The Bible tells us in Galatians 5:6 AMPC that **faith is energized through love. So every time you catch a revelation of the Lord's love for you and kindness toward you, faith is the result.**

Just look at these miracles the Lord Jesus did for people who saw Him in His love and grace, and notice what He said to them:

- A blind beggar, hearing that Jesus was passing by with a great multitude, cried out to Him believing that He would show mercy. Jesus didn't disappoint. He healed the man and said, "Go your way; **your faith** has made you well" (Mark 10:46–52 NKJV).

- A woman who suffered continual bleeding for 12 long years, after hearing about Jesus healing all who came to Him, pressed through the crowd to get to Him. She believed that if she could just touch His garment, she would be healed. And she was. Jesus said to her, "Daughter, **your faith** has made you well" (Mark 5:25–34 NLT).

Friend, every time you see Jesus in His grace, He sees you in your faith! So if you're looking to have more faith today, don't focus on your faith. Just see your Lord Jesus loving you and showing you grace in every area of need. That's when you'll experience the same unstoppable faith that Caleb and John had rising up within you to take every mountain in your life!

OWN THE WORD

Get on YouTube or Spotify and find a cover of the song "Jesus Loves Me" that you like. Take time to listen to it on repeat until you're filled with a sense of the Lord's love for you. As you go about the rest of your day and even step into your tomorrows, practice being conscious of Jesus' deep love for you—whether you're having a good day or not. In fact, practice it especially when you're hit with setbacks and challenges. It's in those moments that you'll really see how having a consciousness of Jesus' love keeps you strong and full of faith!

You can also watch this free sermon **"Becoming the Disciple Whom Jesus Loved"** at JosephPrince.com/gmtm. Scan the QR code to check it out.

READ

Joshua 14:7–8 / Mark 10:46–52
Mark 5:25–34

JESUS LOVES YOU.

BASE CAMP 4

OWN THE PROMISE

LEARN HOW TO *HOLD OUT* FOR EVERY BLESSING AND BREAKTHROUGH, ESPECIALLY WHEN THEY SEEM SLOW IN COMING.

PIT BULL . . . WELL, ALMOST.

DAY ONE

GET GOD'S BEST. DON'T SETTLE FOR LESS

Have you ever seen an American pit bull terrier latch on to a bone, a piece of clothing, or anything for that matter? Once he gets his teeth in something, he's not letting it go without a fight.

The reputation of this canine's powerful and unrelenting bite so precedes it that many believe its jaws are outfitted with a locking mechanism that clamps them down so tightly you need a stick to pry its mouth open. Truth be told, the pit bull's jaws are not physiologically different from any other dog's. When it comes to bite strength, there are other dog breeds with drastically stronger bites. But what *really* sets the pit bull apart is its *psychological* makeup. A pit bull is hardwired to bite and not let go.

When it comes to the things of God and owning His promises for our lives, God wants us to have that same "pit bull" tenacity to lay hold of that which

He has already given us. He wants nothing less than for us to possess our possessions—every good thing that Jesus died on the cross to purchase for us!

But so often, when we're confronted by contrary situations, when bad reports come streaming in, when we don't see our breakthroughs for a protracted period of time, it can be so easy to buckle, roll over, and settle for less.

Think about the circumstances in life you've just gotten used to. Maybe there was a time you used to believe God for an answer or breakthrough, but as the weeks and months went by and nothing changed, you just learned to accept the way things were. You learned to resign yourself to feeling unfulfilled at work, waking up to that pain in your body, or living with that endless stream of negative thoughts. You learned to depend on the advice you find on Google or YouTube to cope with your situation. And you learned to tell yourself to be satisfied with the other things in life you've got going for you because they're "good enough," and you shouldn't hope for too much more.

But do you really think that's God's best for you? To settle for the natural advice or compromises the world has to offer?

Here's the thing about settling: it doesn't stop where you think it does.

Settle once and you'll easily find yourself settling again.

And again. And again.

Every time you settle, you actually end up with less.

And less. And less.

It's a slow, insidious process of compromise mingled with disappointment and doubt that eats away at your confidence in a good God and erodes your inheritance until before you know it, you're left with nothing. And here's the scary thing: we convince ourselves that we're okay with it.

Friend, *it is not okay.*

It's not okay to settle for a life of pain when Jesus already bore your sickness. It's not okay to settle for a life of lack when at the cross, Jesus was made poor for your sake so that your needs might be fully supplied. It's not okay to settle for a life of anxiety, depression, and stress when Jesus wore the crown of thorns to redeem you from every mental oppression. It's not okay to settle for a life of "good enough" when God gave up heaven's *best*, Jesus, His beloved Son, for you!

Now if there's one person who knew anything about not settling for less and who had an almost "pit bull faith" when it came to believing God, it has to be the guy whose audacious claim you see on the cover of this book! Incidentally, did you know that Caleb's name actually means "dog" in Hebrew?

Let's think for a moment about Caleb's journey. He first laid eyes on his mountain when he was 40 and finally took it when he was 85. That's 45 years of waiting. That's twice as long as some of you have been alive. And here's the most mind-blowing thing: Caleb, at the end of those 45 years, was still strong, passionate, hopeful, and refusing to settle for anything less than what God had promised him.

How is that possible? For most of us, it just takes a couple of months, if not weeks, before we feel discouraged and begin resigning ourselves to our "lot in life." But not Caleb. He reveals his secret to faith and patience in what he said to Joshua at the end of those 45 years. He went up to his oldest friend and recounted the journey they had taken together:

> "**You know the word which the LORD said to Moses the man of God concerning you and me in Kadesh Barnea . . . 'Surely the land where your foot has trodden shall be your inheritance and your children's forever**, *because you have wholly followed the LORD my God.' And now, behold, the LORD has kept me alive, as He said, these forty-five years, ever since the LORD spoke this word to Moses while Israel wandered in the wilderness; and now, here I am this day, eighty-five years old.* **As yet I am as strong this day as on the day that Moses sent me; just as my strength was then, so now is my strength for war, both for going out and for coming in.** *Now therefore, give me this mountain."*
>
> *—Joshua 14:6–12* NKJV

Did you catch the first thing Caleb said to Joshua? He quoted what God had promised them both all those years ago—verbatim. He didn't mumble some vague idea of what God had promised, but he quoted it word for word. Like a pit bull with its viselike grip on its prey, Caleb bit into what the

Lord had promised him and doggedly refused to let it go. Through all his years of waiting, he kept and guarded God's word in his heart like his life depended on it!

The result? **The divine promise that Caleb kept in his heart kept him.** At 85 years old, his heart was as filled with faith and his body as charged with strength as when he was a young man! It was as though God suspended time for him so age couldn't catch up to him and disappointment, jadedness, and resignation couldn't touch him.

And here's the best part: at the end of those 45 years, Caleb had a revelation of and experienced the Lord's faithfulness and miracle-working power in his body and soul that he wouldn't have if he hadn't taken the journey of faith to believe God and hold out for His promise.

Friend, the Lord wants you to see this: **while settling brings you to a place with far less than you started with, faith will always bring you to a place with far more than you ever imagined.**

Even if there is a delay, the Lord will compensate for it. 2 Corinthians 4:17 NKJV tells us that "our light affliction, which is but for a moment, is working for us a far more exceeding and eternal weight of glory." I love The Message version, which says, "Even though on the outside it often looks like things are falling apart on us, on the inside, where God is making new life, not a day goes by without his unfolding grace. These hard times are small potatoes compared to the coming good times"!

Caleb must have had a revelation of this, this sure-to-happen, awesome reality that lay beyond all the years he spent in the wilderness. It fueled his faith and caused him to persevere in keeping God's word in his heart.

You can ask God for this revelation too.

Ask Him to open your eyes to see the exceeding good and glory that are waiting for you on the other side of the challenge you're going through. When you see it, just like Caleb, you won't settle for anything less. You'll guard God's Word and promises in your heart and keep pressing in for them! You even have this assurance from Jesus Himself in Luke 11:9 NLT: "I tell you, keep on asking, and you will receive what you ask for. Keep on seeking, and you will find. Keep on knocking, and the door will be opened to you." By His grace that's constantly unfolding in our lives, we are supplied with the pit bull faith and perseverance to do just that.

KNOCK, KNOCK

OWN THE WORD

James 1:2–5 NKJV narrates so beautifully and succinctly the journey of faith and patience: "My brethren, count it all joy when you fall into various trials, knowing that the testing of your faith produces patience. **But let patience have its perfect work, that you may be perfect and complete, lacking nothing.** If any of you lacks wisdom, let him ask of God, who gives to all liberally and without reproach, and it will be given to him."

Cultivate a habit of faith and patience today. Instead of being quick to give up or throw in the towel when you don't see your breakthrough, practice involving the Lord. Write down a list of prayer requests you want to see happen in your life and begin to confess and pray over them whenever you have some free time. Remember, prayer doesn't have to be long to be effective. Speak to the Lord in your own simple words, asking, declaring, and thanking Him for what He is already doing!

READ

Joshua 14:6–12 / 2 Corinthians 4:17
Luke 11:9–13

← Dive deeper into today's truth.

UNKNOT ME.

DAY TWO

WHERE IS GOD IN THE MIDST OF MY STRUGGLE?

Let's be real. We all have days when reality can seem to contradict God's promises so blatantly and painfully we can't help but wonder, *God, what's going on? Where are You? Where are You in the midst of the struggle I'm facing in school? Where are You in the midst of the challenge I'm dealing with at work? Where are You in the midst of the breakdown in my relationship? Where are You when I need You the most?*

There was a young woman in the Bible who knew exactly what that felt like. If there's anyone who had reason to ask that question—*Where is God?*—it was Esther.

Her story begins with captivity. Esther was born many years after the Israelites were delivered from Egypt but when they were once again under the rule and persecution of another people. And this time, it looked like God wasn't showing up at all. Read the book of Esther through and through, and you won't find His name. Not even once. Not even when a nationwide law was passed to destroy Esther and her people. Not even when evil people in power planned to sabotage and kill Esther's closest family. In the moments when Esther needed God the most, it looked like He was nowhere to be found.

It was a gut-wrenching, heart-sinking feeling. One that you might be familiar with.

But before you lose hope and throw in the towel, you need to know this: **while you might not see God showing up in the way you think He's supposed to, He is more present and active than you realize.**

Although we never find "God" or "the LORD" in the book of Esther, we find in the original Hebrew text the letters of His name, *YAHWEH* (יהוה), hidden as an acrostic in pivotal moments of the story.

Before we get into that, here's a short plot synopsis:

Esther's story goes from beauty pageant to impending genocide real quick. Almost as soon as her beauty steals the king's heart and he makes her the new queen, Esther discovers the plot to annihilate her people. She finds out that the king, having been influenced by his murderous advisor, Haman, signed off on a decree to massacre all Jews on an appointed day (Est. 3:13 NKJV). Face to face with a potential holocaust already set in motion, Esther has to decide whether to hide her identity or risk her life by pleading her case before the king. And it's no small risk—it's punishable by death to approach the king without being summoned (Est. 4:11 NKJV). Queen or not, Esther isn't exempt from this law. And the king seems to have no qualms about getting rid of his queen . . . he had just gotten rid of his previous one (Est. 1 NKJV)! Yikes.

Remember, as all this was taking place, it looked as if God had checked out and left His people to fend for themselves.

But did He really?

Esther makes up her mind: "I'll go to the king, even though it's forbidden. If I die, I die" (Est. 4:15 MSG). Unbeknownst to the entire nation, behind the blazing bravery of this young woman was a God who was not going to let her down.

When Esther put her life on the line and entered the king's court, God was there influencing the entire situation. We see His name hidden in the conversation that Esther had with the king (read right to left):

> *So Esther answered, "If it pleases the king,* ***let the king and Haman come today*** *to the banquet that I have prepared for him."*
> *—Esther 5:4* NKJV

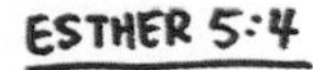

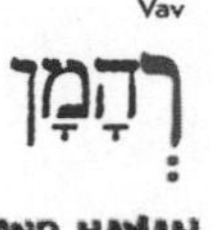

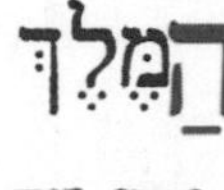

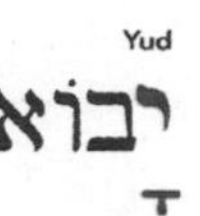

God gave Esther incredible favor with the king so that when she invited him and Haman to her banquet where she planned to expose the evil of Haman's plan and plead for the lives of her people, the king more than willingly agreed to attend.

And when the three of them were at the banquet, God was there too, pulling the strings and backing Esther up. When Esther revealed that she was a Jew and that the murder spree Haman had called for had actually been against her, this was what happened:

> *Then the king arose in his wrath from the banquet of wine and went into the palace garden; but Haman stood before Queen Esther, pleading for his life, for he saw that* **evil was determined against him** *by the king. When the king returned from the palace garden to the place of the banquet of wine, Haman had fallen across the couch where Esther was. Then the king said, "Will he also assault the queen while I am in the house?"*
>
> *—Esther 7:7–8* NKJV

Talk about perfect timing. Perfect timing that God orchestrated to make sure this evil man never saw daylight again. We know this because God's name is hidden, once again, in this climactic confrontation:

Isn't that amazing? At the end of the day, the Jews were not only preserved, but they also destroyed all those who insisted on attacking them (Est. 9 NKJV). Because of their great victory, the day of their would-be genocide became a day of celebration that they called Purim, which Jews all over the world still celebrate today. They went from having no chance of surviving to absolutely thriving because the Lord was right there with them, working behind the scenes to turn everything around for their good.

So to answer your question, *Where is God in the midst of my struggle?*, He is right there in the thick of it. Romans 8:28 NLT says, "God causes everything to work together for the good of those who love God and are called according to his purpose for them." Friend, maybe you can't see Him working in your situation, but He is there all the same, even risking you being disappointed with Him so that He can orchestrate everything to work together for your good.

Do you know why, of all the names He goes by, the one He chose to hide in Esther's story is *YAHWEH*? Because ***YAHWEH* means "promise-keeping God."**[1] You see, the Lord wants you to know without a doubt that He remembers all the promises He's made to you in His Word, and He will make sure they come to pass.

Do you know why you can be sure, absolutely sure, of it?

Because He's written His name, that same name *YAHWEH*, in your story too. We talked about how His name appeared in Esther's story at pivotal moments **but none of those moments compare to the moment in *your* story where His name appeared.** It appeared above His head when He was nailed to the cross, arms outstretched, all the while thinking of you. The Bible records that when Jesus hung on the cross, there was a sign hung over His head written in Hebrew, Greek, and Latin that read: "Jesus the Nazarene, the king of the Jews" (John 19:19 YLT). While the scripture in its original Greek language only reveals the Greek wording, I believe the Hebrew translation would have been ***Y**eshua **H**aNazarei **V**eMelekh **H**aYhudim*. And here we see God's name, *YAHWEH*, appear as an acrostic once again, signifying that at this crucial moment, the Lord intervened in your life and guaranteed a life of blessings and breakthroughs for you.

Like we said in Week 1, the cross is not just a picture of a promise made, but also of a promise kept. This is why you can be sure, without a shadow of doubt, that He keeps His promises to you.

Friend, it's easy to see His fingerprints in our lives when we look back after our trials are over. But let's be people who believe that the Lord is always working in our lives, even and especially when it looks like nothing's happening. Just because we know and believe deep down in our gut He really is who He says He is—our promise-keeping God.

Footnote

1. Martin, Jenna. "7 Meanings of Yahweh and Why It's Such an Important Name for God." Bible Study Tools. Accessed April 16, 2020. https://www.biblestudytools.com/bible-study/topical-studies/why-it-matters-that-god-is-yahweh.html.

OWN THE WORD

Psalm 119:105 KJV tells us that God's Word is a lamp unto our feet and a light unto our path. This means that beyond the visible situations around us, He can give us divine insights into what He is doing behind the scenes in our lives.

Think about your own challenge in the light of the story of Esther. What are the points and moments in Esther's journey that you can identify with? How does it look like in the natural? And what do you think God is orchestrating on your behalf and for your good in your own situation? Write them down in your journal and commit them to the Lord in prayer.

READ

The book of Esther / Romans 8:28

KEEP BURNING.

DAY THREE

DISAPPOINTMENT-PROOF FAITH

Confused, disappointed, and discouraged. That's how 2 of Jesus' disciples felt as they trudged away from Jerusalem and all the madness that had taken place in the city that past week. *The supposed Messiah crucified by the Romans? How could that be? Wasn't He supposed to be the one to save Israel?* It seemed like there was nothing left for them to do but give up hope and head home to Emmaus.

Have you ever found yourself in such a place in your journey of faith? Confused because things didn't work out the way you thought they would. Disappointed because you thought God would show up in a certain way and He didn't. Discouraged because it looked like there was nothing left for you to do but leave your worn-out faith behind and carry on with life as best as you could.

It's at this exact moment, when Jesus' disciples were feeling this way, that Jesus showed up. Disguised as a stranger and fellow traveler, He walked alongside them and casually asked them what was wrong. So they told Him, essentially, that their faith had been misplaced. What they had been hoping for—that their nation Israel would be redeemed—didn't happen. This Jesus, the supposed Messiah, didn't come through.

How do you think Jesus responded to them? Do you think He used this moment for His "big reveal" so that He could watch them keel over in shock at the divine plot twist?

Nope. That's what you and I might have done, but not our Lord Jesus. Instead of giving them a quick fix for their disappointment and discouragement by revealing that He was very much alive and well, Jesus took the opportunity to give them the secret to resilient, disappointment-proof faith.

Do you want to know what it is?

This is what He did: for the next few hours, "**he carefully unveiled to them the revelation of himself throughout the Scripture.** He started from the beginning and explained the writings of Moses and all the prophets, showing how they wrote of him and revealed the truth about himself" (Luke 24:27 TPT). That's right, the whole time He continued walking with them to Emmaus, He kept His physical identity hidden and instead revealed Himself in the Bible! Starting at Genesis, He shared with them how the stories in God's Word whispered His name and the prophecies echoed His irrefutable love, grace, and great sacrifice.

Now why did He do that?

Because He was showing them (and us) that **disappointment-proof faith is all about fixing our eyes on Him and not just the outcome we desire.**

You see, the real reason we get overtaken by disappointment and discouragement is not that things don't work out the way we want them to. It's *really* that somewhere along the way, **we start letting what we *want* eclipse what we *know* about the Lord**—His faithfulness, His love, His power that's always working behind the scenes for our good.

That's why it's so important that we actually know Him in the first place! If not, we end up only using our faith for the specific outcomes we want, and we let those outcomes determine for us whether He's good or not. That, my friend, is disappointment-*prone* faith. And that's why we end up discouraged, giving up, and even walking away from church, just like the 2 disciples who walked away from Jerusalem where all the other disciples were gathered.

What Jesus did for them on the road to Emmaus was to shift their focus back on what *really* mattered—Him. Luke 24:15 NKJV tells us that He "drew near and went with them," even walking 7 miles away from Jerusalem where they were supposed to be, and dealt with their disappointment by reminding them of **who** their faith was placed in—how trustworthy, reliable, and true to His Word He is. It's only at the very end of their journey, when they asked Him to stay the night with them, that He revealed Himself physically to them, and they realized who they'd been walking with the whole time!

After this incredible encounter with the Lord, the two disciples were so freed of disappointment, their hearts so warmed, and their bodies so reinvigorated that they walked all the way back to Jerusalem and shared the encouraging news with the others!

What's interesting is what they said to each other: "Didn't our hearts burn within us **as he talked with us on the road and explained the Scriptures to us?"** (Luke 24:32 NLT). Notice they didn't say their hearts burned within them when Jesus revealed Himself to them in the flesh? It was when He revealed Himself to them in the Bible!

Friend, if you've ever found yourself wishing that Jesus would just appear to you in person and speak to you about everything you're upset about, He wants you to know **it's more important that you see Him in the Scriptures than in the flesh.** Everything you need to know about Him and everything He has to say to you is in the Word of God that you hold in your hands. Today, by His Spirit that lives in you, He is still revealing Himself to you in the Word and longs to have a personal walk with you down your own Emmaus Road.

But the Bible is so thick, I don't know where or how to start.

The best way to start is to understand that every book and every chapter is meant to point you to Jesus. The Bible is a love letter from Him to us that helps us understand His heart for us and what He's done for us. **Jesus is the key to unlocking every truth in Scripture.** That's why in the early church, the people always heard the apostles encouraging them to get to know Jesus better (2 Pet. 3:18 NIV, Eph. 1:17 NIV)! So regardless of what chapter and verse you flip to, ask the Lord to show Himself to you. That's how you have your own personal walks with Him down Emmaus Road and allow Him to lead you in a life of disappointment-proof faith!

OWN THE WORD

Having disappointment-proof faith doesn't mean you'll never feel disappointed or discouraged again. Remember how we talked about the fact that faith is not a feeling in Week 3? Disappointment-proof faith is faith that *withstands and outlasts* disappointment, and it can be built by looking past your disappointments and taking them as opportunities to see the Lord afresh.

So are you disappointed about an area in your life? Bring that area to the Lord, open your Bible, and ask Him to show you more of Himself and bring your focus back to Him. A great book in the Bible to start with is the gospel of John. In it, you'll see the divine character and personality of the Son of God, your loving Savior, as He went about preaching and teaching, healing and helping all who came to Him.

READ

Luke 24:13–34 / The book of John

← There's more here!

"I'LL HAVE A DOUBLE."

DAY FOUR

DESIRING DOUBLE

How many times has your weekly screen time report popped up on your phone and surprised you?

Total screen time: 29h 8m

Daily average: 4h 9m

Instagram: 33%

YouTube: 22%

Twitter: 17%

TikTok: 13%

Snapchat: 9%

Facebook: 3%

Bible App: 3%

And that's not even counting the time you spend binge-watching Netflix at home.

Isn't it crazy what an accurate reflection our online consumption pattern is of this generation? This generation lives and breathes content. We create and consume it at a rate unlike any other. It's become muscle memory for us to take out our phones and start scrolling multiple times a day before we even realize that's what we're doing. Looking for entertainment, knowledge, and inspiration, we spend hours scrolling through social media, streaming videos, taking BuzzFeed quizzes, shopping online, playing mobile games . . . all in a bid to satisfy a deep hunger inside that we often confuse with "boredom" or conveniently excuse as a need to "unwind."

While that might sometimes be the case, more often than not, this chronic restlessness and hunger we feel are pointing us to something deeper—a hunger within that the endless scrolling, streaming, shopping, or gaming *cannot satisfy.*

Here's what the One who created you wants you to know: **that hunger and desire on the inside of you can only be satisfied by Him.**

Ecclesiastes 3:11 NLT tells us that when God made us, He "planted **eternity** in the human heart." This means you're not just a body and a mind with thoughts and emotions. There's more to you than that. God has put eternity in you, and it's called your **spirit**. Our spirits are the most important part of us, and yet in a world that inundates our senses with endless choices of entertainment, we so easily go through life ignoring it. And so we end up being **stuffed with content and yet spiritually starved.**

Well today the Lord wants to show you a divine menu He's prepared for you that will really feed and fill you.

Before we get into it, I should warn you that partaking of what's on this menu will result in a few things. You won't just be spiritually fed, satisfied, and fulfilled. **You will also be equipped and empowered by the very presence and power of God to live an impactful, purposeful, meaningful, and extraordinary life.**

The Bible tells us of a man called Stephen in the early church who was spiritually fed and filled (Acts 6:5–15 NKJV). He was full of faith and the Holy Spirit, full of God's grace and power. And the result? He performed amazing miracles and indisputable signs among the people that showed God was real and moving among them. When unbelievers started questioning and debating with him, they were not able to resist or stand against the wisdom and the Spirit by which Stephen spoke. When those in power started to feel threatened by Stephen's influence, they hurled false accusations at him and brought him to court, and all the judges couldn't help but stare at Stephen in awe as his face shone with the unmistakable glory of God.

This is what happens when your spirit is full. You start operating and functioning in your daily life at another level. You start living a life full of faith, grace, and the power of the Holy Spirit. You start seeing God's miracle-working power working in you and through you. You start acting and speaking with irresistible wisdom. You start being a lighthouse of God's glory for everyone, even your unbelieving friends, to see.

Okay, are you ready?

Here's what's on the Lord's menu to fill your spiritual appetite:

The anointing of God

What's that? **It is the presence of the Holy Spirit—Jesus' own Spirit—that brings with it the supernatural power and ability of God.** In the Old Testament, every time the anointing of God came upon a person, they moved beyond the limits of their natural abilities and *even their personalities* to carry out great and mighty exploits for the Lord. In the Old Testament, we see how Gideon was transformed from a timid young man into a judge and leader of Israel who boldly rallied the people against the innumerable army of the Midianites (Judg. 6 NKJV). Samson became so strong that he snapped bonds of ropes that were holding him down like they were flax, and picking up the jawbone of a dead donkey, he single-handedly slew 1,000 Philistines (Judg. 15 NKJV). David killed Goliath and became someone known to prosper in everything he set his hands to (1 Sam. 17:51; 18:14 NLT)!

Now isn't that something worth desiring and seeking out that is better than just sitting around being entertained and updated about other people's lives? In fact, here's what the Lord wants you to know about His anointing: **you can ask for more of it.**

That's exactly what one man in the Bible, Elisha, did. He was so hungry for the anointing of God that he asked for a **double portion** of it. Not only did he ask for it radically, but he also pursued it radically with his master, the great prophet, Elijah. Yes, the same Elijah we spoke about in Week 2 who did awesome signs and miracles no one had seen before.

Now if we were Elijah's apprentices, most of us would say that being even half as anointed as our master would be good enough for us.

But not Elisha. He desired double of what Elijah had.

You see, Elisha knew it was the Lord Himself who had anointed Elijah, **and the Lord always had more to give.** So when it was Elijah's time to pass the baton to him and Elijah asked him, "Ask! What may I do for you, before I am taken away from you?", Elisha responded without missing a beat, "Please let a double portion of your spirit be upon me" (2 Kings 2:9 NKJV).

Now that was a bold request. Even Elijah himself was slightly taken aback and said, "You have asked a hard thing. Nevertheless, if you see me when I am taken from you, it shall be so for you; but if not, it shall not be so" (2 Kings 2:10 NKJV).

As we've seen time and again throughout Scripture, **God loves bold requests.** So watch what happened. *Almost immediately* after Elisha made his request, as teacher and apprentice continued their walk, "suddenly a chariot of fire appeared with horses of fire, and separated the two of them; and Elijah went up by a whirlwind into heaven" (2 Kings 2:11 NKJV). It was almost as if the moment Elisha said he desired a double portion of the

Lord's anointing, the Lord said, "Okay, I'll make sure you have it! There's no way you're going to miss seeing Elijah go!"

Friend, that's how the Lord responds to you when you desire and ask for His anointing to be upon you. That's how eager He is to fill you with His Spirit!

By the anointing of God, Elisha went on to perform 16 miracles as compared to Elijah's 8, exactly twice the number. These included resurrecting a boy from the dead, healing a man of leprosy, purifying poisonous water, and multiplying barley loaves to feed hungry people. All because the Lord met him that day and poured out a double portion of anointing on him because he so desired it!

That's the heart of your Father God for you. He loves you, and it's always in His heart for you, His beloved child, to have the best. **In fact, the very reason He wants you to desire His anointing and even ask Him for more of it is so that He can lavish it on you!**

This is exactly what Caleb's daughter, Achsah, found out about her father's heart. Yes, she was the daughter of the man whose bold and audacious faith we've been reading about over the last few weeks. She too went boldly to her father and said, "Give me a blessing; since you have given me land in the South, give me also springs of water." And Caleb, because of his great love for her, **gave her the upper springs and the lower springs** (Judg. 1:15 NKJV).

Now get this: springs in the Bible are a picture of God's anointing (John 4:14; 7:37–39 NKJV). The upper springs are a picture of the Spirit of God *upon* us in power, just like how it came upon the heroes in the Old Testament. And the lower springs are a picture of the Holy Spirit residing *in* us as believers today, guiding us in our daily lives.

Because Jesus made us righteous by His blood, we not only get to have the Holy Spirit *upon us* like Gideon, Samson, and David, but **we also get to have His powerful anointing dwelling *within* us to teach and guide us in ALL things!** Look at what 1 John 2:27 NLT says: "But you have received the Holy Spirit, and he lives within you, so you don't need anyone to teach you what is true. For the Spirit teaches you everything you need to know."

Wow, that's a double portion right there! And it's our Father's gift to us, ours for the taking.

Now how do we take this powerful anointing that God is supplying? Friend, we need to understand that **God's anointing is not just a thing, but it's a person, and His name is Jesus, the Anointed One!** We increase in anointing by desiring more of Him, by taking time to seek and soak in His presence, and by simply beholding and appreciating the beauty of His grace. The more conscious we are of His presence that dwells in us and goes with us wherever we go, the more we will see His anointing flow in our lives.

David, king of Israel and one of the most anointed psalmists in the Bible, puts it this way about the inestimable value of the presence of the Lord:

> *"**One thing I have desired** of the LORD,*
> *That will I seek:*
> *That I may dwell in the house of the LORD*
> *All the days of my life,*
> *To **behold the beauty of the LORD,***
> *And to inquire in His temple."*
> *—Psalm 27:4* NKJV

May these beautiful words of David about the **one thing** that he desired and sought after more than any other thing be etched in our spirits and become the one pursuit in our own lives too.

Let's move on to the next thing on God's menu:

A deeper revelation of His grace

In the times we're living in, the Lord is constantly serving us more and more of His grace through technology. And He does it in a really practical way. He's made the message of His grace so readily available for us to partake of, as available as Instagram, YouTube, Facebook, Twitter, and every other app we tap on by muscle memory. His messages and words of grace are *literally* on these platforms! Now more than ever, we have access to online church services, sermons, and worship sets that carry His sweet presence, that bypass the mind and go straight to the spirit.

You see, the Lord knows we are people with a voracious appetite. In fact, He actually made us that way. As people of grace, we are the Benjamin

Generation (Benjamin was the youngest brother of Joseph, who is a picture of our Lord Jesus. Joseph's first words to Benjamin in Genesis 43:29 NKJV were, "God be **gracious** to you, my son"). As the Benjamin Generation, this is how the Lord describes us:

> *"Benjamin is a* ***ravenous wolf;***
> *In the morning he shall devour the prey,*
> *And at night he shall divide the spoil."*
> *—Genesis 49:27* NKJV

We, the Benjamin Generation, are likened to "a ravenous wolf." It's no surprise that we have a voracious appetite, an insatiable hunger. But what is the "prey" we're really after? Wolves are often found going after **lambs**—a picture of Jesus, the Lamb of God, at the cross. So what we're really craving for is the gospel of grace!

The truth is that we can never get enough of it. The gospel is not a story we hear once and put away on a shelf. Romans 1:16 NKJV tells us that **the gospel of Christ is the very "power of God to salvation for everyone who believes."** The word *power* actually means "strength, ability, power for performing miracles, moral power and excellence of soul, the power and influence which belong to riches and wealth, power and resources arising from numbers, power consisting in or resting upon armies, forces, hosts."[1] Take time to read that again and realize that every time you feed on the gospel of grace, you're receiving that kind of supernatural power into your life!

No wonder the Bible says that the Benjamin Generation has 5 times more than all the rest. In Benjamin's story, he received 5 times more changes of clothes and 5 times more food from his brother, Joseph. This is a picture of us receiving from Jesus **5 times more changes of anointing** (different abilities and skill sets to function in different roles, e.g. student, creative, businessman, author, producer, church volunteer, etc.) and **5 times more natural and spiritual foods!**

Friend, like Genesis 49:27 NKJV says, let's choose to "devour the prey" (feed on the gospel of grace) so that we will be able to "divide the spoil" (activate the power imparted to us to bless others). Instead of filling all our time, our minds, and our emotions with content that doesn't make a whole lot of difference in our lives, let's feed and fill our spirits with the anointing of God and desire a deeper revelation of His grace.

And let's not stop there but always ask for double!

Footnote

1. NT: 1411, James Strong, *Biblesoft's New Exhaustive Strong's Numbers and Concordance of the Bible with Expanded Greek-Hebrew Dictionary*. Copyright © 1994, 2003, 2006 Biblesoft, Inc. and International Bible Translators, Inc.

5 TIMES MORE.

OWN THE WORD

The anointing of God

Since God's anointing is all about having the Spirit of the Lord with and in us, the way we draw out more of His anointing is to **practice being conscious of His presence.** Take time to talk to Him like a friend. Have conversations with Him as you go about your day. The more you value His presence in your life and cultivate a deep consciousness of being in a relationship with Him, the more you will see His glory and anointing manifest in your life!

A deeper revelation of His grace

We're spoilt for choice. There are so many incredible preachers of the gospel who frequently post grace-filled content for you to feed on. Make it a point to plug in to some good preaching when you're getting ready in the morning or commuting to or from school or work. If you want some really power-packed, bite-size content, check out my Instagram page or YouTube channel!

READ

2 Kings 2:1–18 / Judges 1:12–15
Psalm 27:4 / Genesis 49:27

IT'S NOT THE END :)

DAY FIVE

FAITH THAT NEVER FAILS, *EVEN* WHEN YOU DO

3 strikes and you're out!

We probably all know how a baseball game works. A batter steps up to the plate with 3 chances to hit a ball from a pitcher. Fingers crossed, he hits it out of the park and gets to circle the bases and reach home safely in one play. But if he swings at a pitch and misses once, twice, three times, he's out of the game after 3 strikes!

Maybe you don't care much about baseball, but have you ever felt like you've struck out *in life*?

Just think of all the times you committed to yourself or to others that you would do something, and then failed to come through. And worse still?

When you're given the chance to make amends, to start again, to do over, you strike out then too.

Too many strikeouts and we can feel like giving up. Even when things start looking good or taking a turn for the better, the fear of failing or messing up can weigh heavy on our minds, trapping us in fear and dread of that impending moment when something somewhere falls apart because we can never keep it all together.

Friend, are you afraid that the things you still haven't figured out, solved, or fixed in your life are going to rob you of the promises of God? Even as we near the summit of our journey, are you worried that your faith will peter out at the very last moment when it counts the most?

If there's someone in the Bible who can relate 100% to petering out when it counts the most, it's none other than Peter.

Loud-mouthed, brash, speaks first and thinks later, Peter is the very picture of someone who can never keep it together for long. One moment he's walking on water with his eyes fixed on Jesus, and the next moment he's distracted by the wind and waves and starts sinking and screaming (Matt. 14:28–31 NIV). One moment he's proclaiming Jesus as the Messiah, and the next moment he's bringing Jesus aside and rebuking Him for talking about going to the cross (Matt. 16:13–23 NIV)!

When it comes to #EpicFails, the most epic failure of Peter's life has got to be the time he boldly proclaimed his undying devotion to Jesus and ended up having to eat his words. He started out confident, declaring to Jesus in front of all the other disciples, "Even if everyone else falls to pieces on account of you, I won't." Can you imagine the look of incredulity on the faces of his friends?

And when Jesus responded by telling Peter that that very night (when He would be arrested and begin His excruciating journey to the cross) he would deny Him not once but 3 times before the rooster crowed in the morning, Peter violently protested, "Even if I had to die with you, I would never deny you" (Matt. 26:33–35 MSG).

Now that's the wrong kind of bold faith. That's bold faith in *yourself*, and that never ends well.

Yet for all of Peter's faults, his brashness, and his inability to control his wild tongue, there was just something to love about him—his humanness.

Maybe we've never said what Peter said to the Lord before, but we've all had times when we felt so passionately about something that we made promises we couldn't keep. We've all had moments when we determined in our hearts to do something, only to fail spectacularly. Maybe for you, it's that bad habit you just can't kick, or that standard you set for yourself that you just can't live up to. Maybe it's a decision you promised yourself and others you would stick to but keep compromising on over and over again, each time feeling like you let yourself and everyone else down.

That's exactly what happened to Peter. At the worst possible moment to fail, when it counted the most, Peter failed.

Not once.

Not twice.

But thrice.

Strike 1: as Peter sat around a fire in the middle of a courtyard a short distance from where Jesus was being held, a servant girl called him out for being one of Jesus' followers. Instantly, Peter denied it, answering her, "Woman, I don't even know him" (Luke 22:57 NLT).

Strike 2: another person looked at him and called him out as well, and Peter retorted, "No, man, I'm not!" (Luke 22:58 NLT).

Strike 3: someone else recognized his Galilean accent and said he was in Jesus' squad, and this time, Peter blew up. With cursing and swearing, he spat, "Man, I don't know what you're talking about" (Luke 22:60 NLT).

At that very moment, the rooster crowed, and all Peter heard was, *"3 strikes and you're out!"*

It's not hard for us to put ourselves in Peter's shoes and imagine how he must have felt. We've all been there. We're all familiar with the intense guilt, shame, and sinking feeling of letting people down.

We're also familiar with the frantic thoughts that follow, thoughts and worries about what people must be thinking about us for having failed. But how did *Jesus* feel about Peter at that moment? What was going through His mind after witnessing one of His closest disciples betray Him over and over again in the span of just a few minutes? And all while He was enduring the ordeal of being interrogated and knowing He would go to the cross?

Surely He must have felt angry, offended, and gravely disappointed to say the least.

That's what Peter must have thought too.

That is, until he actually locked eyes with Jesus at the very moment when he thought he had struck out for good.

Luke 22:61 NLT tells us that "at that moment the Lord turned and looked at Peter." It wasn't a look that said, "I knew it. I knew you'd fail Me." It was a look that said, "Peter, **hold steady. I still love you.** Remember what I told you?"

Wait, what? What had Jesus told Peter before this? Luke 22:32 AMP tells us that when Jesus predicted Peter's denials, He also assured him, "I have prayed [especially] for you [Peter], **that your faith [and confidence in Me] may not fail; and you, once you have turned back again [to Me], strengthen and support your brothers [in the faith].**"

That's what Jesus wanted Peter to remember the moment he failed, that he would come out stronger because of it and even be able to strengthen others. Can you believe it? When Peter utterly blew it, Jesus didn't change His good opinion of him, but believed that he would come out stronger and become a testimony. Jesus still believed the best of him. Jesus still loved him exactly the same and saw his failure as a chance for him to experience a new measure of His grace.

Friend, that's the same way the Lord feels about *you* when you blow it, when you have a lapse in judgment, when you blindly follow your emotions, or when the weakness of your flesh takes over. **Jesus still believes the best of you.** He never dishes out guilt, shame, or warnings about how close you were to striking out. He only dishes out grace, and it's this unexpected abundant grace that causes us to break free from sin and come out stronger!

This is how crazy gracious Jesus is: when Peter failed, Jesus did everything He could to make sure it was *impossible* for Peter not to see His heart of love for him. You'd think that Peter is the one who should have tried to win Jesus back after betraying Him, but it was Jesus who took the time and effort to win Peter back when he was wallowing in guilt and condemnation.

On the day of His resurrection, He left a message for His disciples telling them where He would be and **specially mentioned Peter** so that Peter would know He still cared for him (Mark 16:7 NLT). On the same day, before He met the rest, He reached out to Peter and comforted him privately so that Peter wouldn't be humiliated before the rest (Luke 24:34 NLT). And He saved the best restoration for last, preparing breakfast by the beach for His disciples so that there, in front of everyone, He could restore Peter to ministry (John 21 NLT). With coals of fire burning and possibly a rooster crowing faintly in the background, the scene provided an unmistakable throwback to that painful night. Right there, Jesus affirmed Peter 3 times, one for each time Peter had denied Him. This is the same Jesus we have rooting for us and restoring us when we fail!

You see, in our weakest moments, it is the Lord who holds on to us. It is His faith that never fails. Not the other way around.

When Peter experienced Jesus' love for him when he failed, he was strengthened and transformed beyond anything he could have imagined. From a petrified, guilt-stricken disciple so painfully aware of and crippled by his weaknesses, he became a fearless, confident, convicted preacher of God's Word. Just a few weeks later, he would stand up and preach powerfully to thousands of people and see 3,000 lives come to know the Savior, Jesus.

Jesus.

Jesus, who never gives up on us.

Jesus, whose love and grace strengthen us.

Jesus, whose faith never fails, even when we do.

OWN THE WORD

Just like Jesus made breakfast by the sea at daybreak for Peter and restored him there, He wants to do the same for you. Tomorrow morning, get up a bit earlier to catch the sunrise. You can find a nice spot to watch it happen or you can even watch it from your bedroom window. As you're watching the sky turn from dark to light, signifying a new day and new start, talk to the Lord about an area of your life you feel like you've messed up in. Journal or speak with Him about what happened, and allow Him to speak to you, affirm you, and graciously restore you.

READ

Matthew 26:31–35, 69–75
Luke 22:31–34, 54–62 / John 21

PUBLIC TRANSPORT FOR ALL
COMMUNITY NEED
BEFORE PROFIT
THE CLIM
IS CHANGIN
WHYAREN'T W
STRONGER
TOGETHER
SAVE
THE
EARTH

DAY SIX

ON MISSION

If you're not angry, you're not paying attention.

Ever heard this quote before? You probably have, and some of you even wear it proudly on your T-shirts. It's a statement that lets everyone know you're woke and tells them straight up that they should be woke too. They should be aware of the social injustice happening all around the world. They should be aware of our planet going up in flames. They should be aware that *no, we have* not *reached a time in modernity where we are beyond improvement.* And we should all make a difference and fight for what's right.

This generation has got a rep for being the most socially, politically, and environmentally conscious generation there ever was. As a whole, we believe in activism, and we believe that we have the power *and the onus* to change the world for the better. We've made it our mission!

If you think about it, that's the one mountain many of us have set our sights on—the mountain called Utopia, where we achieve a better world.

First of all, you'll be happy to know the Lord is *extremely* woke and He, too, fights for the causes of the oppressed and powerless. Proverbs 15:3 NKJV tells us that "the eyes of the LORD are in every place, keeping watch on the evil and the good," and Proverbs 16:11 NLT makes it clear that "the LORD demands accurate scales and balances." Throughout the book of Proverbs, we see how He does this. In Proverbs 22:22–23 NLT, we see how He defends the poor and the needy from those who would take advantage of them. In Proverbs 23:10–11 NLT, we read how He guards and protects orphans who can't fight for themselves. If that's not enough, the whole book of Proverbs ends with chapter 31, which says in verse 8–9 NLT, "Speak up for those who cannot speak for themselves; ensure justice for those being crushed. Yes, speak up for the poor and helpless, and see that they get justice."

That's how much God cares. That's the heart He has for people.

And yet **that's not the mission He's given us.**

After Jesus rose from the dead, He met His disciples on a mountain and gave them this message instead:

> *"But you shall* ***receive power*** *when the Holy Spirit has come upon you; and* ***you shall be witnesses to Me*** *in Jerusalem, and in all Judea and Samaria, and to the end of the earth."*
> *—Acts 1:8* NKJV

Did you get that? With the power of the Holy Spirit given to them to make any kind of dent in the universe that God would, the disciples were given but one mission: to be witnesses of Jesus to people all over the world. That's the mission given to us today too.

Why is it not to make poverty history, or destroy all oppression, or heal the planet?

Because the Lord sees the big picture, and He knows that everything broken in this world is born out of the brokenness of the human heart. Some of us blame capitalism and consumerism for the state our society is in. Others blame the greed and selfishness of the people in power calling the shots. But the truth is that everything corrupt and depraved in this world goes back to the corruption and depravity of the human heart. The human heart doesn't just need to be fixed, it needs to be *replaced*.

And the only One who can do that is Jesus.

Ezekiel 36:26–27 MSG gives us a beautiful picture of what happens when a person gets saved. The Lord says, "I'll give you a new heart, put a new spirit in you. **I'll remove the stone heart from your body and replace it with a heart that's God-willed, not self-willed.** I'll put my Spirit in you and make it possible for you to do what I tell you and live by my commands."

Friend, the answer to really making a difference in the world is to save its people. It's to spread the message of the good news of Christ and make disciples out of all nations. When people's hearts are changed, their actions, speech, and everything about their lives will change as a result (Prov. 23:4 NKJV). Of all the causes we can fight for, don't you think this is the greatest?

Of course, there's nothing wrong with fighting for the causes you believe in, but don't forget the big picture: save the world's people and the world will be all right.

Most importantly, this mission we've been given is not short-sighted, focused only on the here and now. This mission has eternity in mind. The difference we make in the lives of those we bring to Christ goes far beyond their years on earth. It gives them an eternity with the Lord in heaven. At the end of our days, there's only one thing we get to take with us: precious souls whom Jesus gave His life for. There is no difference we can make in someone's life that's more meaningful than introducing them to the Savior!

So will you team up with the Lord and take on this mission?

That's right, Jesus wants to partner with you. Mark 16:20 TPT says that "the apostles went out announcing the good news everywhere, **as the Lord himself consistently worked with them**, validating the message they preached with miracle-signs that accompanied them!" Do you see how the Lord didn't just give us this mission and leave us to get it done on our own? The relationship He wants with us when it comes to doing this great work isn't that of a general and foot soldiers, but that of co-laborers! That's

why 1 Corinthians 3:9 NKJV, KJV explicitly calls us "God's fellow workers" or "labourers together with God."

Friend, this is a powerful partnership with the Lord unlike any other. It's a different kind of partnership than the one where He helps you with your school work or your career progression. In this partnership with eternity in mind, you get a special portion of His miracle-working power and grace. Acts 4:33 NKJV records that "with **great power** the apostles gave witness to the resurrection of the Lord Jesus. And **great grace** was upon them all." In this partnership, the Lord supplies you with abundant, mighty, overflowing power and grace that manifest in undeniable supernatural results for the unrivaled purpose of reaching the hardest people with the love of God and advancing the gospel of grace.

This is also a beautiful partnership with the Lord because you're aligning your heart and mind with His. No longer are you simply asking Him to do things for you (even though there's nothing wrong with that), but you're making His desire, His plans, and His purposes your own. You're sticking close to Him and working with Him, hearing His heart of love for others, discovering what He's passionate about, gaining His perspective on things, and setting your sights on the mountain He's set His sights on.

You see, our mountains aren't just about our inheritance, our promises, our breakthroughs, our blessings, our turnarounds. In Psalm 2:8 NLT, the Lord encourages us, "Only ask, and **I will give you the nations as your inheritance**, the whole earth as your possession."

Friend, don't bypass the mountain with the giant sign that says "SOS—Save Our Souls." Don't set your sights on every other mountain and mission in the world and miss this one. Ephesians 1, which tells us our inheritance in Christ, also reveals our place in this world: **"The church, you see, is not peripheral to the world; the world is peripheral to the church. The church is Christ's body, in which he speaks and acts, by which he fills everything with his presence**" (Eph. 1:22–23 MSG). When we align ourselves with God's purposes and say yes to partnering with Him, we become the most effective and powerful world changers we can ever be!

OWN THE WORD

Sometimes, before we change the world, the Lord empowers us to change *our* world. Think of the people in your life who have yet to know Jesus. It could be your parents, your sibling, or one of your best friends. If you find it hard to share the gospel with them because you don't want to pressure or alienate them, remember that you're not doing this alone, and that the Lord is always with you to create opportunities for you to speak to them and give you the right words to say. Pray and ask Him to lead you in the best way to share the good news with them or invite them to church.

Or you can consider passing this book on to them when you're done! If *Give Me This Mountain* has impacted you, let someone else be impacted by it too. Get a copy for a friend or loved one, especially if you feel like it contains truths and revelations that you know will help them. You can also be a blessing by simply getting the word out. Snap a pic of your favorite day in the book and post it on social media with a caption sharing how it spoke to you and hashtag it **#GMTM28**. Together, we can reach more people with the life-changing and *world-changing* good news of Jesus!

READ

Matthew 28:18–20 / Psalm 2:8
Ephesians 1:20–23

← There's more to learn here.

LOVE

DAY SEVEN

THE HIGHEST MOUNTAIN

What is the highest mountain in the world?

For most of us, the name *Everest* immediately comes to mind.

Its summit, reaching nearly 29,035 feet above sea level—the cruising altitude of a jumbo jet—is the highest point on this entire terrestrial landscape we call Earth. The mountain itself is located in one of the most inaccessible and isolated places on the planet, on the crest of the Himalayas, straddling the border between Nepal and Tibet. Up till the late 1960s, it was only accessible by foot or on the back of a yak.

Not only is Everest inaccessible, it is also inhospitable. Apart from the treacherous terrain, the way up is fraught with many perils—risk of sudden storms, avalanches, icefalls, and the human body's finite capacity to endure such extreme altitudes.

With temperatures plunging to nearly -76°F (-60°C) near the summit, coupled with highly volatile and erratic weather, one has to always be vigilant. Even on a good day, gales of hurricane proportions can whip up in a matter of minutes. Past the 26,247 feet mark, in what is known as the "death zone," the atmosphere is so thin and the air pressure so low that it significantly reduces the body's ability to breathe in oxygen, putting any climber at incredible risk of irreparable pulmonary and cerebral damage, extreme frostbite, and in many cases, death.

Yet since its confirmation as the world's highest peak in 1852[1], it has been the inimitable pining and ambition of many an adventurer to reach its summit and leave humanity's mark on the literal top of the world.

Some 100 years later, after numerous failed expeditions, sacrificial loss of lives, and countless attempts thwarted by the sheer magnitude of the task, one man, Edmund Hilary, and his Sherpa, Tenzing Norgay, on a fine spring day in 1953, at long last reached its peak.

Now, compared to Everest, Mount Moriah in Israel at a mere 2,520 feet above sea level doesn't even come close in the running for the highest mountain.

Mount Moriah? **Why does it even matter?**

Well, you see, it was on this mountain that God first called a man out on one crazy mountain expedition. One that would have a deeper and more significant effect on mankind's history and future than even that of Hilary's conquest of Everest. **This man's name was Abraham.**

He first got the brief for this onerous undertaking late one night, when the Lord appeared to him and said, "Take now your son, your only son Isaac, whom you love, and go to the land of Moriah, and offer him there as a burnt offering on one of the mountains of which I shall tell you" (Gen. 22:2 NKJV).

This news hit Abraham like a ton of bricks. Can you imagine the confusion, grief, and sorrow he must have felt as he lay sleepless on his bed that night, pondering within himself what purpose God had in all of this? Finally, concluding that the Lord—his Friend—would not renege on His earlier promises to bless his posterity through Isaac, Abraham made up his mind. He believed that even if the Lord had to raise Isaac from the dead, He would (Heb. 11:19 NKJV)! Early that morning, this man of faith steeled himself, saddled his donkey, and together with Isaac, began the most difficult expedition of his life—the ascent of Moriah.

The difficulty of this journey though was unlike anything faced by the mountaineers on Everest. It did not lie in the terrain that lay before them, nor was it in the sweltering heat of the Middle Eastern sun bearing down upon the small party. Unlike the route up to Everest, there was no physical threat of avalanches or icefalls, no possibility of sudden blizzards, no imminent fear of the ground caving in under them.

And yet, while there was no outward condition that threatened to take them out midway, while there was no zone that threatened to cut off their breathing, **where it *really* took its toll, was *right* there, in the heart of the father.** By now, Abraham's heart was rife with turmoil, the ache that had begun there the night before by this time had amplified into surging stabs of pain. With every step he took, with every foot he placed in front of the other, he felt as if his entire world was crashing down before him. Oh, how his heart must have shattered when Isaac, firewood upon his back and seeing the fire in his father's hands, asked, "Father? The fire and wood are here, but where is the lamb?" (Gen. 22:7 NIV).

"My son, God will provide for Himself the lamb," was all Abraham could muster (Gen. 22:8 NKJV).

There, on the summit of the seemingly insignificant mount Moriah, Abraham, his eyes red and sore from holding back tears, his knuckles white from clenching too hard on the hilt of his blade, his chest quivering with the effort of keeping himself from breaking out in sobs of anguish, prepared to sacrifice his beloved son. He took one final look at the boy, pushing away every memory that came flooding to his mind, lifted up his trembling hands to the heavens, and readied himself to strike.

Then out of nowhere . . .

"Abraham! Do not lay a hand on the lad," He heard the Lord say. He turned around, shaking in relief, and there before him, was a ram caught in a thicket by its horns—the sacrifice provided by the Lord (Gen. 22:11–13 NKJV).

Now by this point in the story, you might be wondering, *What was God's purpose in all this?*

You see, it was never really about Abraham and his sacrifice. It was never really about Isaac, his son. To God, it was a divine picture of what He Himself would do in time to come. **It was always and will always be about His Son, *Jesus,* and *His* sacrifice.**

FIREWOOD.

Almost 2,000 years later, on that same mountain range of Moriah, on a craggy outcrop of rock, on a hill called Calvary, God Himself would, just as Abraham did, **offer His only Son, the Son that He so loved, as a sacrifice for the world.** His Son, Jesus, would conquer the highest mountain, not one measured in feet, but one measured in the magnitude of man's sins and debt piled too high for him to pay (John 16:33 TPT).

In the garden called Gethsemane, it began—this holy ordeal that ended on Calvary's peak. Jesus, vexed to the point of death, sweated blood as His capillaries bled out of His pores. He looked up and asked, "Father, if it is Your will, take this cup away from Me; nevertheless not My will, but Yours, be done" (Luke 22:42 NKJV). The Father, knowing full well that there was no other way for man to be redeemed, delivered to His Son the cup of man's guilt and sin, and with it, the impending wrath it demanded.

And so His enemies came and took His Son. As they would have done to a criminal, they put Him on trial to judge Him. As they would have done to a fool, they dressed Him in fine robes only to mock and beat Him. To make Him an example to those who would follow Him, they bound Him to a post to scourge and whip Him. Yet despite lash upon lash across His back, they could not break Him. Even when covered in blood, still His majesty could not be hidden. No charge could they find, but still they accused Him. They would not be satisfied until the governor at that time, Pilate, condemned Him to die by crucifixion.

Up the rugged path of the Via Dolorosa, the Father watched as they goaded His Son, cross upon His bloodied back as He made His way toward

Calvary's summit. 3 times He stumbled under the weight of His cross—wood for the sacrifice He would accomplish just a distance beyond. To the very cross He carried, they nailed Him, succeeding only because it was He who in love chose to lay Himself down.

There, in the "death zone" on Calvary's bald peak, they hoisted the only begotten Son of the Father on a pole to be taunted and reviled by all who passed by. Unlike Everest, the temperature wasn't anything close to zero, yet He shivered from the effort just to breathe as shock and dyspnea set in, His breath stolen not by the loss of atmospheric pressure, but because of the cruel death contraption on which His full weight now hung.

Yet not a word in retaliation did the Son utter. Instead, He excused their ignorance and freely forgave them all (Luke 23:34 NKJV). So impeccable was His person, despite being completely mangled in form, that even a Roman centurion who witnessed it all couldn't help but mutter, "Surely this man was the Son of God!" (Mark 15:39 NIV).

So there on that mount, we see the wood, we see the Lamb, but where was the fire? Surely there could be no burnt offering without fire.

The pain the Father God spared His friend, Abraham, **He now exacted in full upon Himself—redemption's costly price paid without mercy or quarter.** This time, there was no one there to stop His hand. The Father turned aside His face, letting the fire of a holy God's righteous indignation and wrath fall, unrestrained, upon the true ram of God—Jesus Christ, the Son of God.

Oh, how His heart must have been torn when His Son cried out in anguish, "My God, My God. Why have You forsaken Me?" (Mark 15:34 NKJV), for the first time addressing Him as "God" instead of "Father"! *Yet, He did not relent. He did not show Jesus one shred of mercy or kindness.* On that skull-shaped rock, shrouded by curtains of dark clouds, God unleashed the full force of His fiery judgment—every curse, every disease, every pain, every kind of suffering, every punishment for the entirety of mankind's sin and iniquity—upon Jesus, the perfect sacrifice.

Why, you ask? So that today, when it comes to you and me, He doesn't have one shred of anger or judgment left to dish out. Only **kindness**. Only **mercy**. Only **grace**.

At that moment, as Father, He was never more pleased with His Son's willingness, obedience, and work. As God and Judge, He was never more satisfied by the perfection and efficacy of His Son's sacrifice.

As the prophet Isaiah had penned,

> *"Yet it* **pleased the LORD to bruise Him***;*
> *He has put Him to grief.*
> *When You make His soul an offering for sin,*
> *He shall see His seed, He shall prolong His days,*
> *And the pleasure of the LORD shall prosper in His hand.*
> *He shall see the labor of His soul, and be satisfied.*
> *By His knowledge My righteous Servant shall justify many,*

For He shall bear their iniquities."
—Isaiah 53:10–11 NKJV

At the end of 6 hours, with a loud voice, Jesus cried out, "It is **finished**!" (John 19:30 NKJV). His passion had outlasted the pain. His perfect sacrifice had completely consumed all the judgment. Neither the mountain of humanity's sin nor justice's ensuing wrath could take from Him His righteous life. There on the summit of lowly mount Calvary, like a king, He bowed His head and committed His Spirit back into the loving embrace of His Father.

Jesus, the Son of God, had conquered the mountain. Not Moriah, not Calvary, not Everest, but the mountain of all of man's sin and trespasses—a debt you and I could never ever pay. And together with that mountain, every other mountain that stands in the way of our loving Father's embrace today (Rom. 8:38–39 NLT). By His sacrifice, He satisfied the requirements of divine righteousness and justice, and in mercy paid in full the price for our inheritance—not just eternal life, but also the more-than-abundant life we are to have today.

My friend, this is the reason we can have all boldness and assurance to say to the mountains in our lives, as Caleb did, "Give me this mountain!"

So you ask, "What is the highest mountain in the world?"

Nothing, compared to the mountain our Lord and Savior, Jesus, took for us.

OWN THE WORD

Congratulations! You made it! What a feat!

It has taken us 28 days and 4 base camps to get here. I want you to know that every promise of God for our lives we've learned, every milestone of faith we've crossed together, was first purchased for us by our Lord Jesus at Calvary.

Today take time to look through the book again from cover to cover, and thank the Lord for the amazing grace He has poured out on you and all the things He is still doing and will do in your life.

Lastly, we want to end this book with a powerful visual of what really happened the day Jesus climbed the highest mountain for you. Guard this picture in your heart because it is the unshakable and irreversible reason you can conquer and claim every mountain in every season of your life!

Watch this animation by scanning the QR code below or heading over to JosephPrince.com/gmtm.

READ

Genesis 22:1–19 / Isaiah 53

Footnote

1. Barry C. Bishop, et al. "Mount Everest." *Encyclopædia Britannica*. Last updated April 9, 2020. https://www.britannica.com/place/Mount-Everest.

SALVATION PRAYER

If you would like to receive all that Jesus has done for you and make Him your Lord and Savior, please pray this prayer:

Lord Jesus, thank You for loving me and dying for me on the cross. Your precious blood washes me clean of every sin. You are my Lord and my Savior, now and forever. I believe You rose from the dead and that You are alive today. Because of Your finished work, I am now a beloved child of God and heaven is my home. Thank You for giving me eternal life and filling my heart with Your peace and joy. Amen.

FOLLOW US ON SOCIAL

Connect with us through these social media channels
and receive daily inspirational teachings:

Facebook.com/JosephPrince

Twitter.com/JosephPrince

YouTube.com/JosephPrinceOnline

Instagram: @JosephPrince

WE WOULD LIKE TO HEAR FROM YOU

If you have prayed the salvation prayer or if you have a testimony to share after reading this book, please tell us about it via JosephPrince.com/testimony.

ABOUT JOSEPH PRINCE

Joseph Prince is a leading voice in proclaiming the gospel of grace to a whole new generation of believers and leaders. He is the senior pastor of New Creation Church in Singapore, a vibrant and dynamic church with a congregation of more than 33,000 attendees. He separately heads Joseph Prince Ministries, a television and media broadcast ministry that is reaching the world with the good news about Jesus' finished work. Joseph is also the bestselling author of *The Power of Right Believing* and *Destined to Reign* and a highly sought-after conference speaker. For more information about his other inspiring resources and his latest audio and video messages, visit JosephPrince.com.

ALSO BY JOSEPH PRINCE

Eat Your Way to Life and Health

No More Mind Games

Anchored

Live the Let-Go Life

The Prayer of Protection

Grace Revolution

The Power of Right Believing

Unmerited Favor

Destined to Reign

Healing Promises

Provision Promises

Health and Wholeness Through the Holy Communion

A Life Worth Living

The Benjamin Generation

Your Miracle Is in Your Mouth

Right Place Right Time

Spiritual Warfare

For more information on these books and other inspiring resources, visit JosephPrince.com.